Author
Maryanne Lincoln

Editor
Patrice A. Crowley

Book Designer
Cher Williams

Photography
Impact Xpozures

Illustrator/Assistant Editor
Brenda J. Wilt

Publisher
David Detweiler

Vice President, Stackpole Magazines
Betty Chavez

Rug Hooking ✳ 500 Vaughn Street ✳ Harrisburg, PA ✳ 17110-2220
(717) 234-5091 ✳ (800) 233-9055
www.rughookingonline.com

Contents

Editor's Note

PHOTO COURTESY MARYANNE LINCOLN

Maryanne Lincoln is crazy about color. How else can you explain this story: While she was still hospitalized after the birth of her daughter, Maryanne studied her get-well roses so intently she insisted her rug hooking teacher take one home to develop a matching dye formula Maryanne could use in her next hooked rug.

The point of this humorous episode is not that Maryanne forgot about her baby (nothing could be further from the truth). It's that Maryanne is not kidding when she says she has a desire to duplicate in her dye pot all the colors in the world around her. That unceasing desire to learn about color has led her to a career as a custom dyer, teacher, and writer. Her fame as one of the pre-eminent colorists in the rug hooking community today has also led her to become part of Rug Hooking *magazine's editorial board. Her regular dyeing column in* Rug Hooking *has instructed thousands through the years, as have her classes at rug camps and workshops across the country.*

Just as one of Maryanne's dye recipes can be a perfect blend of hues, Maryanne's knowledge, patience, and wit make a perfect blend for a teacher. I have professionally benefited from her wisdom when I've had a question about dyeing or color. I have also personally benefited from having such a friendly, warm person to work with. So it is with pleasure that I invite you into her dye kitchen, where before long you too will be looking at everything in your world with an eye for color.—Patrice Crowley

About the Publisher

Rug Hooking magazine, the publisher of *Recipes From the Dye Kitchen*, welcomes you to the rug hooking community. Since 1989 *Rug Hooking* magazine has served thousands of rug hookers around the world with its instructional, illustrated articles on dyeing, designing, color planning, hooking techniques, and more. Color photographs of beautiful rugs old and new, profiles of teachers, designers, and fellow rug hookers, and announcements of workshops, exhibits, and gatherings appear in each issue of the magazine.

Rug Hooking has responded to its readers' demand for more inspiration and information by going online, publishing pattern books, revising its *Sourcebook* listing of teachers, guilds, and schools, initiating the Framework Series of in-depth instructional books, and continuing to produce the competition-based book series *A Celebration of Hand-Hooked Rugs. Recipes From the Dye Kitchen* represents but a fragment of the incredible art that is being produced today by women and men of all ages.

For more information on rug hooking and *Rug Hooking* magazine, call or write us at the address on page 1.

Chapter One

Rug Hooking's Magic Ingredient

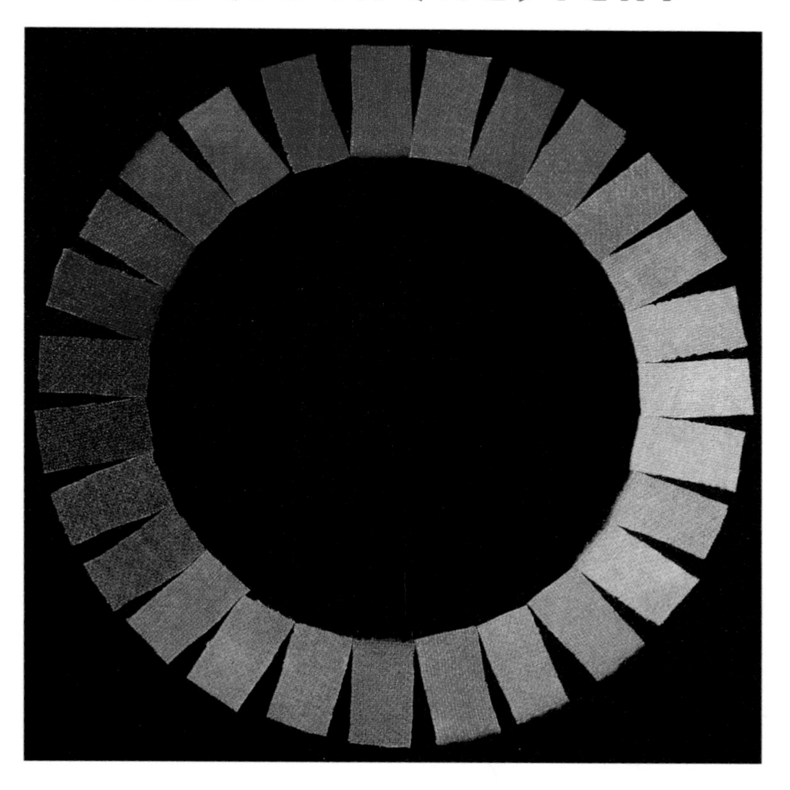

Can you imagine hooking rugs in only black and white? Wouldn't it be boring if we didn't have color to work with? To me, color is the magic ingredient of rug hooking.

Technique may be the most important aspect of learning to hook, but color is certainly the most exciting and flexible. Not long after I began hooking I realized it made great sense to learn as much about color as possible in order to make the most beautiful rugs possible. Once I decided to become a rug hooking teacher, I saw every project that I hooked and dyed for as a teaching tool. So I experimented with color combinations, dye procedures, shading interpretations, and anything else that was applicable. Most important, I was constantly expanding my knowledge of color.

Color is the magic ingredient of rug hooking.

At that time there were not many books available about color. The color course taught by Pearl K. McGown and her book *Color in Hooked Rugs* (self-published, 1954) were helpful, but my curiosity went beyond what I learned from them. I wanted to be able to duplicate the colors that I saw in the world around me.

I decided I would eventually share the knowledge that I acquired, so other rug hookers would not have so many unanswered questions. In the early 1970s I put my notes and experiments together and began teaching a class about color and dyeing. As I have learned new information I have added it to my class notes. Those notes originally only contained information about the Cushing Company's dyes. Now they also include formulas for PRO Chemical & Dye wash-fast acid dyes.

As is the case with almost every rug hooker, I began dyeing wool by following published dye formulas. The formulas made beautiful colors, but I came to find that a red wasn't bright or dark enough for me, or a green was too brassy or dull for what I was hooking. My mind was never quiet about such things. I never seemed to be able to just dye the color as it was written and be completely happy with it. I simply had my own ideas about the colors I wanted in my hooked rugs.

It's a Cinch, 38" x 24 1/2", #4-cut wool on burlap. Designed by Pearl K. McGown. Hooked by Maryanne Lincoln. This was the first rug Maryanne hooked and dyed by herself, with the guidance of her teacher.

A Personal Experience

Color is a very personal experience, and everyone gets pleasure from different colors and color combinations. One of the characteristics of color is its beauty. This beauty trips us up because we want to add it everywhere, and we often add it with abandon. It takes practice to be able to create a color plan for a rug that is as beautiful as its individual hues.

Not all people perceive color the same way. Some of us are limited by a degree of color blindness we are powerless to change. However, most of us just need to awaken or sharpen the color skills we already have.

Some people have an inherent sense for what colors go together, but most of us have to work at it. For instance, after we choose the colors for a rug, we also have to consider the quantity of those colors, as well as their brightness, dullness, lightness, and darkness. Sometimes we do this as we go along, but it is helpful to think about these things before we start to hook.

Understanding Color

When we are trying to decide which colors to hook into a rug, we have to ask ourselves not only if they look right together, but also if they look right against the background we intend to use. How do we know how to select the proper colors and combinations? The answer is to understand color itself, and then apply that understanding by working with dyes. There are principles of color theory that can help us combine and use colors with confidence, but in my opinion they should never be referred to as rules because rules can dampen an individual's creativity. Nonetheless, to creatively work with color we have to use these principles as an outline, and then fill in and modify our color knowledge as we gain experience.

Knowledge and experience comes from actually dyeing hooking wool yourself, so you truly understand all the elements of every color you use and how those colors interact with each other. When you first start to dye, it is nice to stick exactly to a formula or procedure for the first year or two, because the written information helps you develop familiarity with procedures and achieve excellent results. But once you gain experience, you will have ideas of your own about dyeing, and there will be no holding you back. After

***Leaves bellpull*, 6" x 36", #3-cut wool on burlap. Designed by Pearl K. McGown. Hooked by Maryanne Lincoln. Maryanne developed all her own dye recipes for this piece.**

Some people have an inherent sense for what colors go together, but most of us have to work at it.

all, if every dyer always did everything as it was written in dye books, there would never be any new formulas or dye procedures.

If you don't do any dyeing and only use what is available commercially, it is still possible to create beautiful hooked rugs; but you can definitely be more inventive if you put the dye pots on and create colors that are all yours.

An Inexact Science

Dyeing is not an exact science, but its variables help us produce unique swatches and rugs. It wouldn't be fun to attend rug exhibits if we kept seeing the same combinations over and over. The important thing is not that your dyed wool looks exactly like someone else's, but that you get the same results each time you dye.

Dyeing my own wool for my hooked rugs has done more than help me create colorful swatches. It has altered my perception of the world around me. Now I spend time truly observing things, especially when I walk in the woods. I amuse myself by trying to figure out how I might dye a flower stem or tree bark or rock that I've seen. Even at home I take a second look at the blue in a wallpaper pattern or the rose tones in the face of a child or the green of new leaves in spring sunshine. This habit has proved valuable when students ask for special dye recipes for their projects. My years of observations, study, analysis, and experimentation have led me to this book. It can lead you to a colorful world that is more accurately captured in your own hooked rugs.

Chapter Two

COLOR THEORY

***Janelle,* 16" x 16", #6-cut wool on burlap. Designed by Jane McGown Flynn. Hooked by Maryanne Lincoln. Maryanne did the color plan and dyed all the wool for this pillowtop pattern. The background is an antique brown dyed with blue and black over orange wool.**

Visual Understanding

How can we study color to get the most out of it? To get started we need a basic understanding of the three dimensions of color. They are:

HUE	—The color-wheel name of a color, not the fashion-color name.
VALUE	—The lightness or darkness of a color.
INTENSITY	—The saturation or strength of a color, referred to as brightness or dullness. Also known as *chroma*.

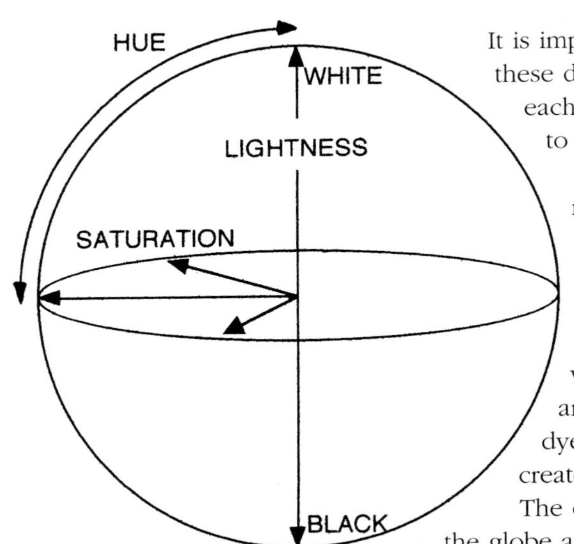

It is important to understand the concept of each of these dimensions as well as how they interact with each other. As you read about color, relax and try to master these basic ideas.

To help visualize the relationships, I like to relate the three dimensions of color to a globe. Think of the north pole as white and the south pole as black. The core between the poles is a gradation of gray from very dark to very light. This represents the scale of values from the darkest up through lighter and lighter values to white. Every color can be dyed in values by using the jar dye method to create a gradation swatch from light to dark.

The equator of our model is the thickest part of the globe and the farthest from the scale of values. All the color-wheel colors march around this belt in order. This is the scale of hues. All hues are mixed by combining the primary colors, which are red, yellow, and blue. If you begin tracing that equatorial belt at red and move around toward yellow, you'll pass through red-orange and yellow-orange. Then you'll go from yellow through yellow-green and blue-green to arrive at blue. Finally you'll move back toward red through blue-purple and red-purple. Now you're back to red again.

Intensity is represented on our earth model by the relationship of the equatorial color-wheel hues to the value scale that

Complementary colors are the key to color mixing and matching.

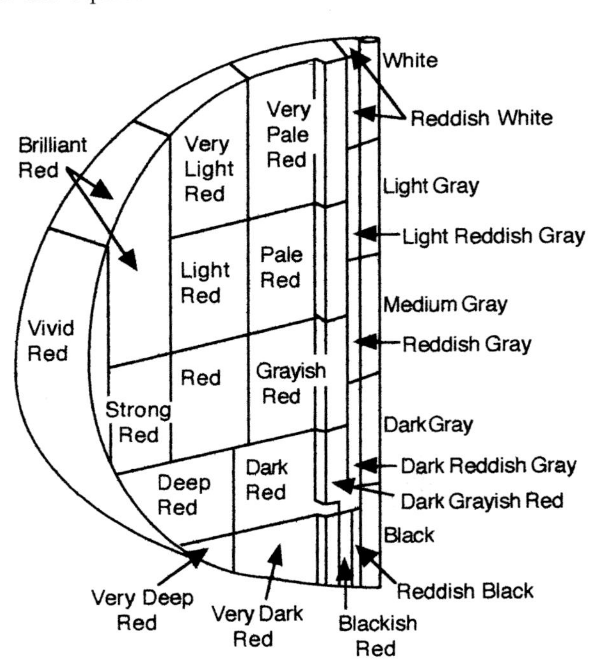

runs through the core from black to white. As we move from the value scale (the core) toward the hue scale (the equator), the intensity of the color gets brighter. If you start at the equator and move toward the core, the intensity of the color gets duller. In fact, if you start at other places on the outer surface of our model and move toward the neutral core the hue gradually dulls and vice versa.

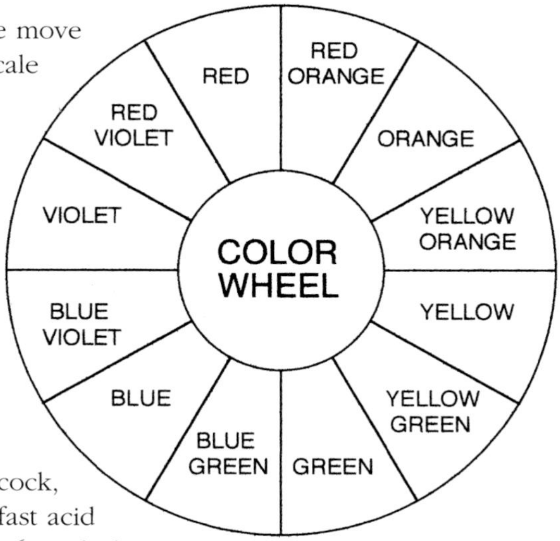

COLOR WHEEL
RED
RED ORANGE
ORANGE
YELLOW ORANGE
YELLOW
YELLOW GREEN
GREEN
BLUE GREEN
BLUE
BLUE VIOLET
VIOLET
RED VIOLET

I have created dye formulas to illustrate these three dimensions of color. I used both Cushing and PRO Chem dyes in the primary colors—yellow, red, and blue—plus dark gray or black. The Cushing dyes are Canary, Cherry, Peacock, and Dark Gray. The PRO Chemical & Dye wash-fast acid dyes are #119 Yellow, #338 Red, #490 Blue, and #672 Black.

When preparing the solutions to dye examples of a color wheel, a gray scale, and an intensity scale, place the dye in a 2-cup glass measuring cup and add a teaspoon or two of tepid water. Stir it, then add 1 cup of boiling water and stir the solution until the dye is thoroughly dissolved. Add warm tap water to bring the level to 2 cups. (Adding the cooler tap water is a safety precaution to avoid the most dangerous part of dyeing—getting burned with boiling water or steam.) I suggest you dye 3" x 12" wool pieces, but to dye smaller ones divide the dye quantities, not the water. For instance, to dye 3" x 6" pieces, measure out half as much dry dye but dissolve it in the same amount of water.

The Scale of Hues

Use the formulas below to dye swatches for a 12-point color wheel showing the scale of hues (the equatorial belt on our globe).

CUSHING	1/8 tsp Canary in 2 cups of boiling water 1/16 tsp Cherry in 2 cups of boiling water 1/16 tsp Peacock in 2 cups of boiling water
	OR
PRO CHEM	1/16 tsp #119 Yellow in 2 cups of boiling water 1/16 tsp #338 Red in 2 cups of boiling water 1/32 tsp #490 Blue in 2 cups of boiling water

To dye 3" x 12" white wool strips you'll add spoonfuls of each of these primary color solutions to jars, then proceed with the jar dyeing steps noted in Chapter 5. Be sure to read Chapter 4 first to have the proper equipment on hand. Each jar that you'll cook the wool in will also contain 1/2 teaspoon of salt and, 30 to 45 minutes into the processing time, 1 tablespoon of white vinegar. Before placing the wool in the jars soak it in a solution of very hot tap water and Synthrapol SP or another wetting agent (see Chapter 4 for more information).

Primary yellow:	12 tsp yellow (use either Cushing or PRO Chem dyes)
Intermediate yellow-orange:	9 tsp yellow + 3 tsp red
Secondary orange:	6 tsp yellow + 6 tsp red
Intermediate red-orange:	3 tsp yellow + 9 tsp red
Primary red:	12 tsp red
Intermediate red-purple:	9 tsp red + 3 tsp blue
Secondary purple:	6 tsp red + 6 tsp blue
Intermediate blue-purple:	3 tsp red + 9 tsp blue
Primary blue:	12 tsp blue
Intermediate blue-green:	9 tsp blue + 3 tsp yellow
Secondary green:	6 tsp blue + 6 tsp yellow
Intermediate yellow-green:	3 tsp blue + 9 tsp yellow

More steps can be dyed between each sample in the chart. The following is a list of additional samples that could be dyed between blue and yellow.

11 tsp blue + 1 tsp yellow	5 tsp blue + 7 tsp yellow
10 tsp blue + 2 tsp yellow	4 tsp blue + 8 tsp yellow
8 tsp blue + 4 tsp yellow	2 tsp blue + 10 tsp yellow
7 tsp blue + 5 tsp yellow	1 tsp blue + 11 tsp yellow

From this list you can calculate the amounts for the other sections of the color wheel. If you dye these additional samples, the total number of samples will be 36.

The Scale of Values

To dye an example of the scale of values, the core of our model, use the jar method discussed in Chapter 5 to dye a gradation of grays over the purest white wool you can find. Dissolve 1/8 teaspoon of PRO Chem's #672 Black in 1 cup of boiling water. Use 3" x 12" white wool and 1/2 teaspoon of salt in each jar, and, after 30 to 45 minutes of processing, 1 tablespoon of white vinegar for each value. It will probably take about 10 values to come out to white.

You can get nearly neutral color by dyeing Cushing's Dark Gray over white. Use 1/4 teaspoon of Dark Gray and dye a gradation as above. If your Dark Gray looks purplish, add 1/128 teaspoon of Canary to it before spooning out the quantities.

As you read about color, relax and try to master the basic ideas.

The Scale of Intensity

The scale of intensity progresses from a gray to a bright color, corresponding to movement from our model's core to a point on the equator. There are 13 samples from middle neutral gray out to bright primary red. To dye these samples follow the steps taken for dyeing the previous scale samples. You'll need 13 jars for this series. First, prepare these solutions:

CUSHING	1/16 tsp Dark Gray in 2 cups of boiling water 1/16 tsp Cherry in 2 cups of boiling water
	OR
PRO CHEM	1/16 tsp #672 Black in 2 cups of boiling water 1/16 tsp #338 Red in 2 cups of boiling water

J Is for Joseph, 34" x 31", #6-cut wool on burlap. Designed and hooked by Patty Yoder. The color plan for this rug is an offshoot of the color classes Patty has taken from Maryanne. With few exceptions each color blends into the one that lies adjacent to it on the color wheel.

Now put one of these dye combinations in each jar:

12 tsp Neutral	5 tsp Neutral + 7 tsp Red
11 tsp Neutral + 1 tsp Red	4 tsp Neutral + 8 tsp Red
10 tsp Neutral + 2 tsp Red	3 tsp Neutral + 9 tsp Red
9 tsp Neutral + 3 tsp Red	2 tsp Neutral + 10 tsp Red
8 tsp Neutral + 4 tsp Red	1 tsp Neutral + 11 tsp Red
7 tsp Neutral + 5 tsp Red	12 tsp Red
6 tsp Neutral + 6 tsp Red	

There's something in particular you should notice about this list of formulas. Look at the total amount of dye in each sample and you will see that it is the same. As one color decreases the other increases by the same amount. Therefore, when you look at the samples, the overall gradation goes from middle gray to red, yet there isn't much value difference between the samples themselves.

Complementary Colors

Now that you are familiar with the rudiments of color theory it's time to learn about complementary colors. Complementary colors are the key to color mixing and matching. Complementary colors—hues opposite each other on the color wheel—dull each other when mixed together. Remembering this fact will help you solve your color mixing problems. So memorize these simple pairs of complements: red and green, blue and orange, yellow and purple. Then remember to use this information. It has become clear to me as I have gained more and more experience working with dyes that this simple information has proven to be one of my best tools.

Sometimes a formula is a bit too bright. Just add a tiny amount of its complement. Other times a formula is not bright enough. Mix it up again and leave out some of its complement. It sounds so elementary, yet it works.

If you limit yourself to developing formulas from red, yellow, and blue, the complement of any one of these three colors is one of the three secondary colors: green, purple, and orange. To put it simply, the complement of any one of the three primary colors is the combination of the other two. For example, the complement of red is green (yellow and blue). The complement of yellow is purple (blue and red). The complement of blue is orange (red and yellow).

This works even when the color is not bright, and it takes a few moments to figure out its components. Just look at a color and decide, in general terms, whether it is red, orange, yellow, green, blue or purple. Take an educated guess. Suppose you're looking at a color we call light oak, a light medium brown. Ask yourself, "What basic color is it?" Your answer will probably be, "Yellow." You know that yellow's complement is purple. So to brighten the light oak remove some of the purple (red and blue) in the dye formula. To dull it, add a small amount of purple. Thus you can develop new recipes by starting with a familiar formula and adjusting its ingredients to get a new color.

Using complementary colors in a color plan is a completely different story. When placed side by side in a rug, complementary colors brighten each other. Even a dull hue can slightly heighten the brightness of its complement. Colors don't have to be particularly vivid to be effective together. In many rugs we combine red roses, mahogany scrolls, and leafy greens on a celery or dark green background.

Finding the Predominant Color

Sometimes it is not easy to identify in simple red, yellow, and blue terms what a color is. Some are just too muddy to easily pinpoint the predominant hue. If it isn't possible, then just manipulate the muddy color until it becomes what you want. In other words, increase in the formula the color that you want, or decrease the complement of that predominant color. If you don't know which color should be predominant, start by eliminating some. Consider each of the primaries and each of the secondaries. Once you have an idea of the predominant hue, you can identify the color that is its complement. Let's say you want blue to be the predominant color in a formula. Add more blue or reduce its complement, which is orange (yellow and red), to take away the ingredient that has been dulling it.

This same concept works when you are trying to match a color and the formula isn't quite right. Break the problem down into manageable steps and work slowly. Consider whether increasing or decreasing the complement will get you closer to a match. Of course, there are many ways that a color can be adjusted slightly.

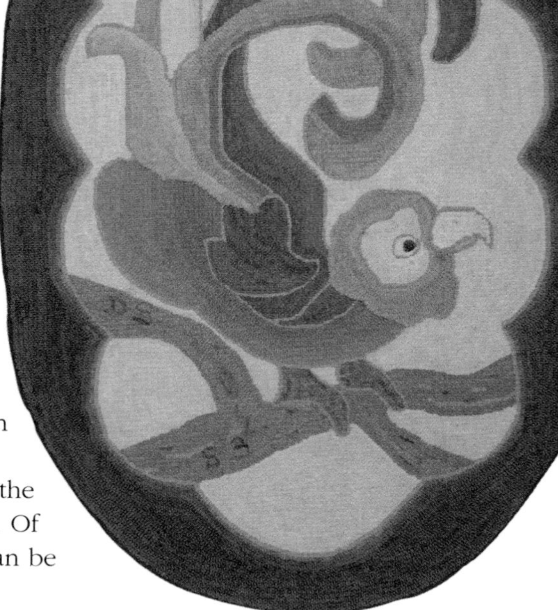

***Polly*, 22 1/2" x 34", #6-cut wool on burlap. Designed by Lib Callaway. Hooked by Diane Stoffel. In this piece Diane used all of the 36 color-wheel hues that she learned about in Maryanne's color course.**

For instance, if you use only one primary color or a combination of two primary colors, the results will be very bright colors as seen on the color wheel. However, when you use the three primaries together, the results will no longer be bright and will depend on how much of the third primary that you add. Try mentally working out a simple combination and then dye it and see if the results are what you expected.

Color-Wheel Rugs

I've included two rugs to show you how some of my students have employed my color theory lesson in their work. *J Is for Joseph* is a wonderfully colorful example of all the hues in the color wheel. A few years ago this rug's creator, Patty Yoder, was in my Texas Rug Hooking Camp color class as an advanced student. As part of that class she dyed the color-wheel samples I mentioned earlier, using PRO Chem dyes. She dyed pieces of wool large enough to hook a project, but I had no idea at the time that she had something in mind. It makes me happy to see all that color so beautifully presented in such an interesting way.

Diane Stoffel was also inspired to hook a rug after taking my color course way back in 1983. She hooked *Polly*, dyeing and incorporating all the color-wheel samples. I knew nothing about her color plan until she showed me the finished rug. Since learning about dyes in that color course Diane has gone off on her own, developing lots of interesting new color variations.

Janelle, which I hooked, gave me a chance to combine materials that displayed analogous relationships. (Analogous hues are those next to each other on the color wheel.) The central motif starts at its base with red and changes to orange and yellow and then back to red at its tip. Notice how I reached into the yellow-greens for a loop or two in certain sections but not in the sections that were primarily yellow. I wanted the yellow to be a resting place for the eye before I shifted color direction back toward red. Also, I was careful to sprinkle bits of these colors in other parts of the color plan. In a small, complex design like this it is often a challenge to get a balanced color plan because of the diversity of motifs.

When I used analogous colors in the greens and blue-greens (as I did with the red to orange-yellow), I played with the hues, always keeping in mind the idea of color placement and balance to please the eye. Finally, just to perk up the yellow a bit, I added some touches of purples, but again red-purple is analogous to red, isn't it? Around and around our eyes are allowed to flow through this delightful design.

PROJECTS

1. If you want to firmly implant this chapter's information in your mind, dye the 36-point color wheel, the gray scale, and the intensity scale. Get together with other interested rug hookers and do the dyeing as a group project. Share the cost, the work, and the samples.

2. Read Faber Birren's book *The Principles of Color* (Schiffer Publishing, 1987).

Chapter Three

WOOL

***Maryanne's Ponies*, 46" x 20", #5- and 6-cut wool on burlap. Adapted from a Patsy Becker design and hooked by Maryanne Lincoln. Maryanne overdyed bright yellow wool for the goldfinch and bright green wool for the background. Other wool was left over from previous projects.**

When I first started hooking, it was easy and fun to find wool remnants for rugs in barrels at local mills. It was even possible to find white and off-white pieces for dyeing swatches. However, these days finding wool can be frustrating because there are not as many sources of an inexpensive supply, and I don't have the free time to scour the countryside for possibilities. If you are resourceful, however, it is still possible to find it in this manner. There are suppliers who advertise in *Rug Hooking* magazine who sell wool by the pound. Also, used clothing can be recycled. Visit rummage sales, yard sales, and thrift shops for used clothing you can take apart and use for hooking.

Nowadays I prefer to buy my wool for dyeing by the bolt and by the yard. It doesn't guarantee consistency of quality or color, but there is a better chance of it, which is important if I should need more of the material later. Each sheep is a unique individual, so it should be no surprise that wool varies from sheep to sheep. Even small differences in the raw wool that a mill uses to weave the yardage that we buy can make a noticeable difference in the results we get from dye batch to dye batch. One hundred percent wool is best for dyeing and hooking, but a blend of wool and a small percentage of nylon will also do well.

Each sheep is a unique individual, so it should be no surprise that wool varies from sheep to sheep.

Cutting Wool

Since I mostly use yardage, I measure 2/3 of a yard (24") and tear it off the bolt. I remove the selvages from the top and bottom edges of the material, then re-fold the material in half, as it was folded on the bolt, so it is double thick. I lay a yardstick on the material from the edge opposite the fold to the fold and snip through both layers in 3" increments. Then I tear the wool at every third snip. A single piece is now 9" x 24". When I dye gradation swatches in batches of 6 swatches at a time, I use 1, 9" x 24" piece of wool in each jar. When it's been dyed and dried I tear it at the other notches, then cut each 24" strip in half. That gives me 6, 3" x 12" strips of each value, which I then collate into swatches. If I plan to dye Color Sheets (my own brand of swatches), I tear the wool at every fourth snip to give me 12" x 24" pieces of wool for dyeing.

Wool for Backgrounds

If I plan to dye for a background, I leave the selvages on the wool to identify the straight of the goods. I cut and hook strips on the straight of the goods, especially when I'm using narrow cuts (#2, 3, and 4).

When figuring out the amount of wool that you need to dye for the background of a rug—the largest area of your rug—you must not only allow an extra bit for shrinkage but also allow an extra bit for the waste that occurs every time you start and stop a strip. More is always better. It's a nuisance to run out of wool

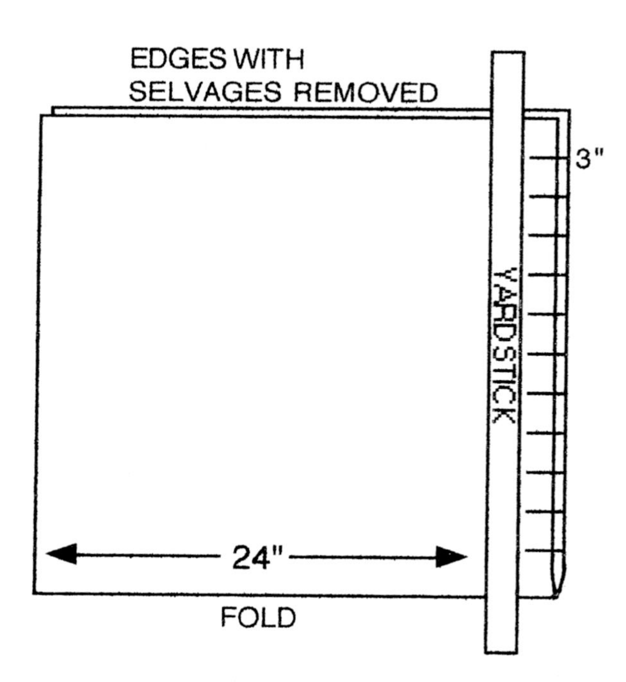

midway through your hooking and have to dye more, especially when you may now be out of the dye or wool you started with. To get the proper quantity of wool for dyeing I multiply the background area by 5. For instance, if the area of the background figures out to be 4 square feet, I dye 20 square feet. Or, you could look at it this way: Allow 1/2 pound of wool per square foot. Therefore, if your rug pattern measures 2' x 3' (6 square feet), you should have 3 pounds of wool.

Wet Wool

There are two properties of wool that you need to consider when calculating quantity and dyeing. First, because of the natural lanolin in it, wool repels water. To get it to absorb water—and dye—we need to add a wetting agent (a detergent) to the soak water and dye bath so the wool will get thoroughly wet. I recommend Synthrapol SP (available from PRO Chem—see the glossary for an address), because I work with it. It will not interfere with the dye process. In fact, it is recommended that you also add a drop or two of it to each dye bath (or each jar if jar dyeing) to help the water and dye fully penetrate the wool. There are other wetting agents available that are also effective, such as Ivory dish detergent.

I use very hot tap water along with a few drops of Synthrapol to wet my wool just before I need it. I don't need to soak my wool overnight because it becomes thoroughly wet in just a few minutes. For convenience, I have an 8-ounce squeeze bottle in which I put 1 teaspoon of Synthrapol and 8 ounces of tap water. I shake the bottle a little to mix the solution and then when I want to add Synthrapol to a soak pot I just put a couple of squirts of this mixture into the pot. If you have hard water, you will probably need a little more Synthrapol than someone who has soft water. However, be conservative at first and add just a little. This will avoid a lot of suds and the necessity of rinsing the wool before putting it into the dye bath. The suds won't interfere with the wool taking the dye, but it is annoying when you heat the dye bath and more suds emerge. If you overdo it, just rinse some of the suds out of the wool before proceeding.

Wool dyes easily. It is amazing how, right before your eyes, wool takes up dye and turns to the beautiful color that you want. But wool will shrink during that process. After all, the dye bath must simmer so the dyes will activate. There is no way to avoid some shrinkage. The amount varies between different lots of wool.

Chapter Four

DYEING EQUIPMENT AND SAFETY

Like any cook about to follow a recipe, you must assemble your tools, pots, and ingredients before you follow a dye recipe. Here's a list of what every wool dyer's kitchen should contain. (Please note: When you're done with these implements, don't throw them back in your kitchen cabinets lest someone pull them out to cook food in. Dyeing utensils and pots should be for dyeing only. *Don't use them for food preparation, as you may end up ingesting the dyes.* Green eggs and ham may be fine for Dr. Seuss, but not for rug hookers.)

ASSEMBLE YOUR TOOLS

- An apron, protective smock, or lab coat.
- 2 pair of rubber gloves. Wear surgical gloves when handling dyes and loose-fitting, heavy, lined rubber gloves for handling hot wool.
- A mask to cover your nose and mouth when you're measuring dry dye.
- Tongs for poking and lifting wool in the dye bath.
- 1- and 3-quart enamel, glass, or stainless steel pots (don't use aluminum, as it will affect the dyeing process).
- An enamel, glass, or stainless steel soup pot (for scrunch dyeing).
- An enamel, glass, or stainless steel roasting pan or canner big enough to hold 6 to 8 quart-size jars (for jar dyeing).
- Small enamel pan to dissolve dyes in.
- 6 to 8 wide-mouth quart-size jars (for jar dyeing).
- 1- and 2-cup glass measuring cups.
- A teaspoon.
- Assorted long-handled spoons for stirring the dye solution in the jars and pots.
- Heavy aluminum foil.
- Dye spoons (see below for more information).
- Plain, uniodized salt.
- White vinegar (5 percent).
- A wetting agent, such as Synthrapol SP (see Chapter 3).
- Wool.
- Dyes.
- A notebook and pen.

As you can see by reviewing the list, the majority of these tools can be found at any kitchen shop. The dye spoons, however, are unique to dyeing and thus will have to be obtained through a rug hooking supplier (see the glossary for addresses). What makes these spoons so special?

A TOD brand dye-measuring spoon is one with calibrated scoops at both ends. One end measures 1/32 teaspoon, the other 1/4 teaspoon. This spoon is what I learned to dye with 30 years ago. I now use and prefer the Grey brand of spoons because a set of three double-ended spoons has scoops that measure 1/128, 1/64, 1/32, 1/16, 1/8, and 1/4 teaspoon. The TOD spoon is adequate for most published formulas. The Grey spoons make it easier to cut formulas down and to dye formulas that have been written after these spoons were introduced. Keep in mind that the fraction with the largest denominator (1/128) is actually the smallest spoon. Likewise, the one with the smallest denominator (1/4) is the largest spoon.

The spoons from both manufacturers are made of polished aluminum. Wash and dry them after every scoop of dye. I don't recommend dipping aluminum spoons in salt to clean them because the salt may eventually corrode the spoons.

Other Means of Measuring Dyes

There are other ways to measure dry dyes and dye solutions besides special spoons and common glass cups. If you measure large amounts of dye for backgrounds and other large pieces of wool, you can get the job done faster and with greater accuracy by weighing the dyes, wool, salt, vinegar, and wool on a scale. Scales are available from PRO Chem (the address is in the glossary). To accurately measure liquid dye solutions, you will have great success with the use of different pipettes, beakers, graduates, and syringes (also available from PRO Chem). PRO Chem has four different glass pipettes for liquid metric measuring: 25 ml (milliliters), 10 ml, 5 ml, and 1 ml. The pipettes each have lines marked out to measure small amounts so that you can be precise down to the drop if need be.

Like any cook, you must assemble your tools and ingredients before you begin.

I use the largest pipette when I want accurate large amounts; in the 25 ml I can measure anything up to 25 ml and then do multiples of it. For instance, if I need 50 ml I fill the 25 ml pipette twice; and if I need 63 ml, I fill the 25 ml pipette twice plus 13 ml. You can measure accurately less than 25 ml in it, but it is difficult to measure amounts less than 5 ml with the 25 ml pipette. The 5 ml and the 1 ml pipettes are more handy for small quantities. For instance, 1.25 ml could be obtained by either filling the 1 ml pipette once plus .25 ml more; or you could use the 5 ml pipette and fill to the 1.25 ml line.

Take time to learn how to use pipettes, beakers, graduates, and syringes before starting to measure dye solutions.

Practice with water a time or two to become familiar with them. See the appendix for metric equivalency charts.

Liquid measurements come in handy when trying to accurately develop substitute formulas. Once you mix up the basic liquids that you will be measuring from, you won't have to handle the dry dyes again until the solution is used up.

Safely Using Chemical & Natural Dyes

Be an informed user: Take the time to read about these dyes before using them.

The dyes we use to color our wool are not toxic, but they are chemicals and should be handled with respect. All of us use laundry and dish detergents, bleach, ammonia, drain cleaners, furniture polish, and the like. They are all chemicals. You should handle dyes with the same amount of respect and care that you handle those products.

If you know or even suspect that household cleaning products irritate your lungs, then always wear a mask when measuring the dry dyes and doing the actual dyeing. Don't have a fan running or a window open when measuring the dry dyes, as the fine particles fly about easily. Do, however, work in a well-ventilated area when actually dyeing to cut down on fumes and steam and have a damp paper towel or newspaper covering your work table to catch errant particles.

If you know or even suspect that household cleaning products irritate your skin, then always wear gloves. The dye manufacturers encourage us to use gloves—and masks—when handling these chemicals.

Neither Cushing nor the PRO Chem dyes come with skull and crossbones symbols on them. But if you have safety concerns, get in touch with the dye company and request a Material Safety Data Sheet.

Ironically, natural dyes may well be more dangerous than synthetic dyes. Some dye plants and mordants (a substance that fixes color in fabric) are poisonous, so be cautious when handling them. There is no company to fall back on for information. It is up to you to learn about them. Don't assume that just because a dye is natural it can't hurt you. Be an informed user: Take the time to read about these dyes before using them.

There are many different classes of synthetic dyes that are used to color textiles. Some are specifically designed for certain fibers. Others are a blend of ingredients so they can be used on a wide range of fibers, from protein fibers like wool to cellulose fibers like cotton. Sacrifices are made when you choose one of these mixtures—sometimes you may not be able to get the color fastness or depth of shade that you want.

Acid dyes are used for dyeing protein (animal) fibers such as wool. Both PRO Chemical and Dye wash-fast acid dyes and Cushing acid dyes are called acid dyes because they need an acidic dye bath to work effectively.

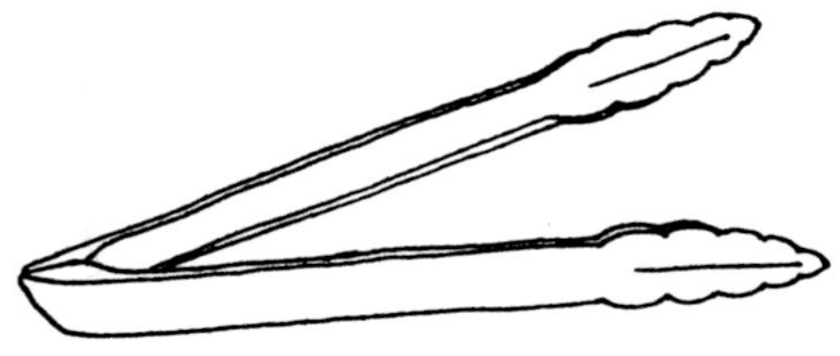

Water, Salt, & Vinegar

Using the proper equipment and procedures will help you dye with perfectly predictable results—if we lived in a perfectly predictable world, that is. We work with a great many variables. Water quality and composition differs from season to season and region to region. Wool varies from sheep to sheep. Dyes have not been consistent over the years. So don't expect consistent results and you won't be disappointed.

Water is not the same from state to state, town to town, or even house to house.

The dye bath starts with a certain amount of water, to which we add small quantities of a wetting agent (discussed in Chapter 3), salt, vinegar, and of course the dyes. All water pretty much looks the same, nice and clear, but the interesting part about it remains hidden, despite that clarity.

Water is not the same from state to state, town to town, or even house to house. It is not the same from season to season—during the wet season the concentration of minerals in it is different from the concentration during the dry season. We can't depend on the potability of water to mean it's OK as a dyeing ingredient. In some parts of the country chemicals are added to community water supplies to alter them for human consumption; those same chemicals (chlorine, for example) can work against us when we dye wool. Then there are those parts of the country where acid rain affects the ground water from which tap water is derived.

Cushing and PRO Chem dyes work best in acidic water, which allows them to attach themselves to wool fibers. We change the acidity of the water and thus encourage that attachment by adding vinegar to the water. We retard the attachment by adding a small amount of salt.

I have always used both salt and vinegar to dye gradation swatches. I add salt to the dye bath before adding the wool to help keep the dye from spotting the material. I add vinegar about three fourths of the way through the dye process or at its end because I like to have dark values that are different from each other, and I don't seem to be able to get those results

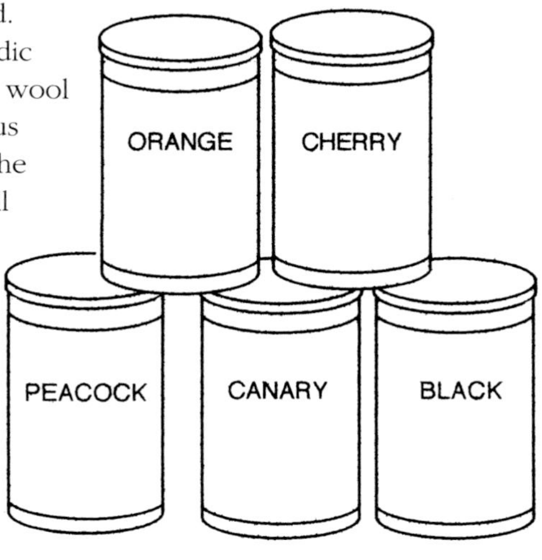

unless I do. Vinegar, or a suitable substitute such as citric acid crystals, is a necessary ingredient in the dye kitchen, not an optional one, when dyeing with acid dyes.

Don't expect consistent results and you won't be disappointed.

Keeping Records

With all your equipment lined up by your stove you are almost ready to begin dyeing. But before you start, make sure you have pen and paper nearby to record your successes so you can repeat them another day. I have a simple spiral notebook to make notes in as I work in my dye kitchen. From those notes I write out a record card and file it so I can quickly retrieve the formula with all its particulars to duplicate later.

I assign a simple name or number to each formula, and then I include all the important information about the swatch: the size and color of the wool, the dye formula, the procedure, a small sample of the results, and any other appropriate comments. I use the back of the card for additional information. Dyeing a lovely color without recording these facts about it reduces your chances of ever dyeing it again.

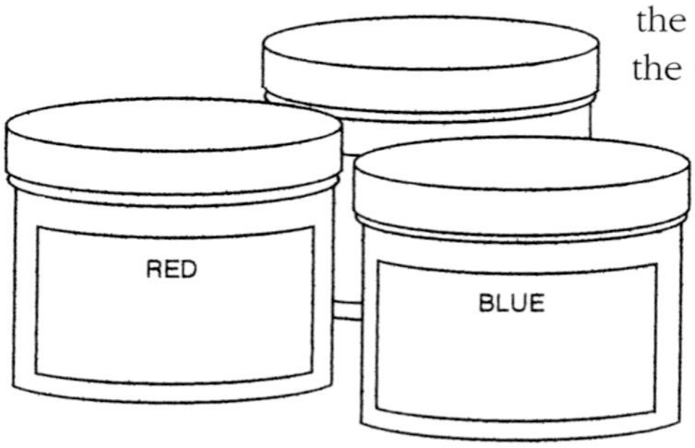

RED

BLUE

Chapter Five

JAR DYEING

***Farmer and Wife*, 32" x 22", #6-cut wool on linen. Designed and hooked by Maryanne Lincoln. Maryanne dyed white selvages blue for this rug's background.**

Before I joined an adult education rug hooking class in 1964, I had had absolutely no experience dyeing anything. During the third class Edna Callis, our teacher, gave a live, complete jar dyeing demonstration. We were expected to go home from that demonstration and dye 8-value swatches right away. We could because on the first night of class everyone had received a notebook of lesson pages that included a jar dyeing instruction sheet. By the time the dye lesson was presented, we were prepared to start dyeing at home. It was the beginning of a long adventure of color discovery for me.

Interestingly, jar dyeing is not the simplest way to dye a piece of wool. However, it is an easy way to dye a gradation of values. At the time none of us in the class even thought to question the procedure. As I recall, I was just excited to be learning how to dye wool for my rugs as well as how to shade flowers and leaves with the swatches that I dyed. If you just want to dye different colors, not gradations, open-pan dyeing is an easier approach (see Chapter 6).

You can't stir your dye bath too much.

The Jar Dyeing Method

Before you begin to dye, read through Chapter 4 to have the right equipment on hand and to take the necessary safety precautions. As a practice run, try the project listed at the end of this chapter.

1. Soak 6 to 8 pieces of 3" x 12" wool strips in hot water with a drop of Synthrapol. If you have hard water, use a bit more Synthrapol. Let it soak while you are preparing the dye bath.
2. Measure your recipe's dry dye formula into a small enamel pan. Add a small amount of cool water to the pan to make a paste. Add 3/4 cup of hot tap water and bring it to a quick boil. Stir. Pour the mixture into a 1-cup measuring cup. Add hot tap water to make 1 cup of solution.
3. Arrange the jars in the roaster. Add hot tap water around the jars until they begin to float.
4. Stir the dye solution and pour 1/2 cup of it into the first jar.
5. Refill the cup with hot tap water to the 1-cup level. Stir and pour 1/2 cup into the next jar. Repeat this process (pouring off half the solution and adding more hot water to the 1-cup level) until all the jars contain solution. You will end up with 1/2 cup of lightly tinted solution after pouring the last value. *Don't pour it into the jar with the lightest solution.* It is not needed for this procedure.
6. Add 1/2 teaspoon of salt to each jar. Then add warm tap water to each jar until each is about 2/3 full. Put a drop of Synthrapol in each jar.
7. Gently squeeze some of the water out of the wet wool. (It is not necessary to rinse it unless you have used a wetting agent other than Synthrapol.) Use tongs to stir the wool into the jars of dye solution. Squish the wool up and down to force the dye solution through the wool. Move the tongs as you work to avoid leaving spots where the tongs grip the wool. Stir the wool often in this manner while the swatches are processing.

Dyeing Multiple Swatches

To dye more than one swatch at a time increase the following: the number of pieces of wool in each jar, the strength of the dye solution, the amount of salt per jar, the amount of vinegar, and the amount of extra water that you add to each jar. For example, to dye one swatch in each jar you'd use the above directions. For 2 swatches per jar you'd double the dye formula, vinegar, and salt per jar, and have enough water in the jar to allow you to stir the wool easily. For five swatches per jar you'd use 5 times the formula, 5 tablespoons of vinegar, and 2 1/2 teaspoons of salt, plus sufficient water to keep the wool submerged.

The amount of extra water is not as important as the size of the material, the strength of the dye formula, or the amount of the salt. I add as much water as I possibly can without overflowing the jars; it is important to add approximately the same amount to each jar.

8 Cover the roaster, *not* the individual jars. If you don't have a cover, loosely cover the pan with heavy foil.

9 Put the roaster over low heat. After about 10 minutes, remove the cover and stir each jar. Turn the heat up to a simmer only—don't let the water heat to a rolling boil. Stir the wool every 15 to 20 minutes. *You can't stir too much.* Make sure each piece of wool is completely submerged before you put the cover back over the jars.

10 Simmer for 1 hour. (When using acid dyes, remove the wool after 30 to 40 minutes and stir 1 tablespoon of white vinegar into each jar. Then put the wool back into the jars. Simmer the wool for 30 minutes longer, stirring it often. Remove the roaster from the heat, let the wool stand in the jars until it cools, then follow the rest of these steps.) Rinse the wool, starting with the lightest value and working toward the darkest. When the water rinses clear, hang the wool to dry. If the water does not rinse clear, put the wool in a small pan with 2 to 4 cups of water and 1 or 2 tablespoons of vinegar. Bring the water to a quick boil. Simmer it for a few minutes or until the water that drips from the wool is clear. If the piece is not one value darker compared to the previous strip, add some of the dye from its jar to the vinegar bath. Be careful, though—it is easy to get it too dark. If you use the vinegar bath for one value, you must do it for every value after that.

11 Clean the jars thoroughly after you've used them to avoid contaminating your next dye project.

Until you gain experience, follow the above jar dyeing instructions to the letter. As you do more dyeing, you will find yourself questioning things and more willing to experiment with dyeing methods.

PROJECT

To hone your jar-dyeing skills prior to dyeing wool for a rug, use the above dyeing method to try one of these formulas on 6 pieces of 3" x 12" natural wool. You'll get a nice orange hue for your efforts.

Cushing
3/32 tsp Cherry +
3/32 tsp Canary
OR
PRO Chem
3/32 tsp #338 Red +
3/32 tsp #119 Yellow.

Chapter Six

OTHER DYEING TECHNIQUES

***Vegetable seed packets*, 11 1/2" x 15 1/2" each, all #6-cut wool on linen. Designed by Florence Petruchik and Maryanne Lincoln. Hooked by Maryanne Lincoln. The antique brown in the backgrounds are discussed in the text.**

There are other ways to dye wool besides the jar method noted in Chapter 5, which is great for dyeing gradations of hues. Open pan dyeing is another method, one that's good for dyeing large pieces of wool of a single value. Here's a warm-up exercise that employs this method.

OPEN PAN DYEING

1. Fill a 1-quart enamel pan half full with hot tap water, and put it on the stove to heat. Fill another, smaller container with hot tap water and a few drops of wetting agent and soak in it a couple of 3" x 12" pieces of light-colored wool (they don't have to be white). Soak the wool while you get the dye pot ready.

2. Choose a package of dye that you would like to try. Open it and measure out 1/32 teaspoon of the dye into a glass measuring cup. Add a couple teaspoons of tepid water to the dry dye and stir it around a little. By now the water in the 1-quart pan should be boiling.

3. Add some of this boiling water to the dye in the glass cup until it reaches the 1-cup mark. Stir the dye solution until the dye has dissolved. Now add it all to the 1-quart pan along with 1/2 teaspoon of salt and one of the strips of wool (the other pieces are to repeat this process for additional practice).

After you've practiced this technique, try using it to dye a 12" x 24" piece of wool. Stir 1/4 teaspoon of dye and 1/4 cup of vinegar in a pot 2/3 full of hot water. Once you put the wet wool into the pot bring the water to a low simmer so it won't boil over. Keep the wool under the water's surface, poking it under when you have to. Continue simmering the water until it clears.

Use half the amount of dye for a lighter value. Use twice as much dye for a darker value. Repeat this dyeing over different colors and sizes of wool. Write down what you do and label the wool when it has dried so that you will remember what you did and what it looked like (wet wool always looks darker than dry wool). This is especially important as you begin to dye over different colors and textures of wool. Keep in mind that the color of the dye formula does not cover up the color of the wool. It adds to it. For instance, if you dye a blue over yellow wool, you will end up with green. If you dye a red over blue wool you will end up with purple.

***Sunflowers in Winter*, 14 1/2" x 19 1/2", #5-cut wool on linen. Designed and hooked by Maryanne Lincoln.**

4 Stir the wool and keep it submerged as much as possible as the water simmers. Cover the pan and let the dye bath simmer for a few minutes. Lift the lid, stir the wool, and adjust the heat when necessary—you don't want a rolling boil.

5 After 5 to 20 minutes add 1 tablespoon of vinegar and stir again to make sure the wool is submerged. Re-cover the pan and continue to simmer and stir the wool often until the dye bath clears. Add a bit more vinegar if the water doesn't clear.

With Cushing dyes sometimes the water won't completely clear no matter how much vinegar is added. A light Cushing dye will clear quicker (in as little as 5 minutes) than a dark one (which may take up to 30 minutes). If there is still color in the pan after 30 minutes, stir the wool once more, turn off the heat, replace the cover, and let the wool cool in the pan—this encourages the wool to take up more dye. Rinse and dry the wool and it will be ready to hook.

Dyeing Backgrounds with Swatch Recipes

Many people dye mounds of wool but never dye the gradation swatches that come from jar dyeing. Therefore, it may seem that jar-dyeing recipes, such as those found in Chapter 8, are useless to them. But that's not true. You can use them for large projects, such as dyeing for backgrounds.

The easy way to dye a background with a formula written for swatches is to just mix up the formula as written and use the open pan method. Spoon the formula into a dye bath with 1/4 cup of vinegar added and place in it a 1/4- or 1/2-yard piece of material. You must have enough water in the pot to accommodate the wool. If it is a little crowded in the pot, that just means the wool will come out slightly mottled. If you want a very light value of the swatch color for a background, cautiously add dye. Put a little in and let the wool take it all up, and then add more if you want it darker. Remember that the wool will look darker when it is wet, so don't stop dyeing too soon. Try to compare the wool in the pot to a wet sample of the color you want. If

Pear flashcard, **9" x 10 1/2", #3- and 6-cut wool on burlap. Designed and hooked by Maryanne Lincoln. Maryanne scrunch dyed the wool for this pear.**

you use all the formula, mix up more and continue until you get the color you want. Repeat the process until you dye enough wool for your background.

There is an easy way to adjust swatch recipes into recipes for dyeing 1/2- and 1-yard pieces. Use the following chart to translate the swatch recipes into the amount of dyes that you need.

VALUE OF SWATCH	1/2-YARD BACKGROUND	1-YARD BACKGROUND
Darkest	4 x the formula	8 x the formula
Next dark	2 x the formula	4 x the formula
Middle dark	1 x the formula	2 x the formula
Middle light	1/2 x the formula	1 x the formula
Next light	1/4 x the formula	1/2 x the formula
Lightest	1/8 x the formula	1/4 x the formula

If the recipe has tiny amounts of dye quantities in it, making it impossible to measure 1/2, 1/4, or 1/8 of the dry dye formula, then mix the whole formula in 1 cup of boiling water and use 1/2, 1/4, or 1/8 of that liquid to dye the wool.

When you are dyeing large quantities of wool be sure your pot is large enough to hold both the wool and enough water to keep the wool submerged. If your pot isn't the right size, divide the total amount of wool into manageable quantities and divide the total amount of dye solution in the same way. Let's say you need to dye 4 yards of material, but your pot will only comfortably hold 2. First mix up enough dye solution for 4 yards, then use half of it to dye 2 yards. When the water has cleared and the color has set to your satisfaction, dye the other 2 yards of material. (Don't forget the vinegar—pour in 1/4 cup each time you prepare a new bath.)

Whenever you have to dye large amounts of wool for a background you always run the risk of not having the pieces match. So many things can alter a color that you must work slowly and deliberately. Think through the entire process before starting so you don't skip a step with one of the pieces. Sometimes you just have to try different things until the color comes out right.

Complements will transform poisons—colors that are extremely bright—into treasures.

Poisons, Treasures, & Antiques

Many bright hues of wool can be changed into beautiful rich dark backgrounds by adding the right dye. Complements (remember your color theory lessons?) will transform poisons—colors that are extremely bright—into treasures. Here are some

***Wentworth Antique*, 56" x 32", #6-cut wool on burlap. Designed by Ruth Hall. Hooked by Maryanne Lincoln. Maryanne used a mottled background for this rug.**

examples: Turn bright turquoise-green into a great black-green background by adding red and black. Turn electric-blue into a dark blue with orange dye. Turn kelly green into a dark dull green-black with red and black dye. Turn bright orange into dark dull rust with blue dye. Turn bright purple into dark dull eggplant by adding red, to make it more red-purple, and then by adding red-purple's complement—yellow-green.

Another means of transforming a troublesome piece of wool into a fabulous background is by overdyeing it into an antique hue (so called because its appearance mimics the hues of old rugs).

The term *antique black* means different things to different people. I usually associate it with a green-black that is unevenly dyed. Other rug hookers think of it as a faded black. Then there are those that consider it a black that has been dyed over grays and beige until it is dark, but not coal-black.

In other words, antique black is a dark color that's truly black in only a few places. If you try to dye it and the color gets dark but not dull enough, remember that complementary colors dull when mixed together. A medium gray wool needs more black to darken to an antique hue. A black-green wool like Dorr Mill's #44 requires red to darken it. Chartreuse or orange in strong portions will do the trick with black wool. Experiment with different wool and dyes, starting with 1 teaspoon of formula per yard and adding it gradually to the dye bath.

My antique brown can be seen in the backgrounds of the vegetable seed packets on page 28. I used blue dye first, and then black over a medium-dark orange-brown piece of wool. If I had had a camel-colored piece and had wanted to age it, so to speak, I could have put it in a blue and black dye bath and it would have taken on a greenish cast, more like antique black than antique brown. Putting red in with the blue before adding the wool to the bath would have dulled the camel and made it browner.

Keep in mind that the color of the dye formula does not cover up the color of the wool. It adds to it.

Mottled Backgrounds

Antique colors can look mottled (or mooshy, as I like to say). So how do you deliberately achieve uneven dyeing? Take a 1/2 yard of wool off the bolt, or about 1/2 pound of wool if you use recycled wool, wet it in hot water with a wetting agent, and dye it in a pot of water (and 1/4 cup of vinegar) that slightly crowds the wool yet allows you to push the wool under the surface of the bath. Poke the wool under the water occasionally, but—and here's the important part—don't stir constantly. This lack of agitation will allow the dye to mottle the wool. Once the simmering water clears, remove the wool and check the color. If you like it, put the wool back in the pot and simmer it a few minutes longer. If you don't like it, add more of the same color or even add another color, then return the wool to the dye bath. Poke it around a little and let it take up the dye.

Scrunch Dyeing

Most of the fruit and vegetable swatches I have developed, dyed, and used in my hookings have been done with a technique I devised that I call scrunch dyeing. I used scrunch dyeing in my *Sunflowers in Winter* rug, in my pansy mat, and in my vegetable seed packets (see the photographs). I use both Cushing and PRO Chem dyes for this type of dyeing. By working with a formula step by step, the color builds in layers.

To scrunch dye you don't need jars or big soup pots; you just need a single 1- or 2-quart enamel pan. Bigger is not better in this case because you want the wool to be crowded in the pan when you dye it.

As always, start by soaking the wool in hot tap water with enough Synthrapol to saturate the fabric. Mix the dye formula in 1 cup of boiling water. Fill the dye pan about 1/3 full with hot tap water. Pour 1/4 cup of the dye solution into the pan. Add 1 tablespoon of vinegar to the bath each time you add 1/4 cup of dye solution. Bring the dye bath to a boil and keep it simmering.

Without rinsing it, remove the wool from the soaking pot. Squeeze out a little of the water so the wool doesn't drip all over the place. Grip the wool with tongs about halfway down its length so both ends of the wool will enter the dye bath simultaneously.

Wool looks darker when it is wet, so don't stop dyeing too soon.

Gradually lower the wool into the boiling (not rolling) dye bath, going deeper and deeper. When the wool will not go any deeper, twist it and, at the same time, scrunch it down until it is completely submerged. The water should have begun to clear just as you do this.

The most important thing to remember when scrunch dyeing is simple: Don't allow enough dye bath for the pieces of wool to be easily submerged. At the same time, there must be enough water so that when you scrunch down hard, you can force the wool under the water without having it overflow. You know you have enough dye bath when you release the downward pressure on the wool and the wool springs back to rise above the surface of the water.

If you want darker wool, add another 1/4 cup of dye and repeat the process. For interesting effects, add two or three different dyes to each batch. I like to use three related colors. Don't mix them together; add one, dip and scrunch, then add another, and so on (that's what I meant about building layers of color). Cover the pan and simmer the wool until the water clears and the color is set. Dark colors must simmer longer than light colors. Rinse, dry, and hook.

Once you get to know various dyeing methods, and combine that knowledge with what you've learned about color theory, you are well on your way to creating beautiful hues for beautiful rugs. But there's more to learn; the next chapter is full of tips to make dyeing easier for old pros and less intimidating for timid beginners.

***Pansy mat,* 22 3/4" x 15 1/4", #3 cut wool on burlap. Designed by Florence Petruchik. Hooked by Maryanne Lincoln. The peach, leaves, cherries, and the brown of the checkered border were scrunch dyed.**

Chapter Seven

TIPS & REASSURANCES

***Collinot*, 36" x 52", #4-cut wool on burlap. Designed by Jane McGown Flynn. Hooked by Ronnie Roisman. Ronnie, one of Maryanne's students, dyed some of the darker hues in this rug to 12 values.**

When you've been dyeing and teaching and learning for as long as I have, you collect a lot of handy information about methods and materials. You also collect a lot of fears from students who believe the world will come to an end if they don't do things exactly the way they've been told to do them. This chapter is a grab bag of reassurances and revelations for both new and old dyers.

Smooth Dyeing

If you are unable to get smooth, even dyeing when jar dyeing, please consider the following suggestions. You'll find that temperature and agitation are the keys to good results.

Water temperature plays a big role in achieving an even spread of dye. Use hot tap water (not boiling water) in the roasting pan around the jars; and don't have heat on under the roaster while you get your jars loaded with dye, extra water, salt, and wool. Yes, it is necessary to use boiling water to dissolve the dye formula, but after it is dissolved use only hot tap water to refill the measuring cup each time. Furthermore, the presoak water for the wool shouldn't be boiling. Hot tap water will do fine.

Next, remember to add extra water to each jar—as much as the jar will allow without overflowing when you stir the wool. After I pour the dye solution into all the jars, I usually add water until the jar is about 2/3 full before adding the salt and then the wool. Stir and slosh each wool strip in its jar as soon as you put it in, and when you move on to the next jar, make sure the wool strip that you just finished working with is under the surface of the solution. The wool can't take up the dye if it isn't down in the solution. If there is still room for water, add it up to the bottom of the neck of the jar where the threads start. At this point, put the roaster, with jars all full, on medium-low heat. In 5 or 10 minutes go back and lift the lid of the roaster and stir the wool in each jar, raising the heat under the roaster if the water in it isn't simmering.

***Sunset Sheep*, 7 1/2" x 5 3/4", #3- and 5-cut wool on burlap. Designed and hooked by Maryanne Lincoln. Maryanne used open pan dyeing for the wool in this little piece.**

However, don't be impatient. If you are having trouble with splotchy wool, it is better to start the batch slowly and bring the heat up gradually, even if you have to process the wool for more than the usual 1 hour. All these little things can add up to more even dyeing.

There's another reason wool can end up spotted. If you don't stir enough, the contents of the jar will not be evenly heated. The wool on or near the bottom of the jar will get hot first, and since dyes activate at high temperatures, that part of the strip will grab the dye first. Therefore, stir frequently and thoroughly.

I am a nervous stirrer. Every time I pass the stove I lift the dye pot lid and stir. Don't feel restricted by the procedure step that says stir every 15 or 20 minutes. That is the minimum amount you need to do to be successful. When I get spotty swatches it is usually because I was distracted and didn't stir enough.

It's also important to stir the wool right away after adding the vinegar. Usually I add the vinegar and stir each value immediately, then stir again 5 or 10 minutes after that. When I turn the heat off I stir each value again and then again in 10 minutes while the wool is cooling, for the wool keeps taking up dye as it cools. Can you see what I mean by saying I'm a nervous stirrer?

I am a nervous stirrer. Every time I pass the stove I lift the dye pot lid and stir.

Matching Colors

If you can't match a color that you originally dyed yourself, a couple of causes could be the culprit. The obvious reason is that the dye itself has changed. This is especially likely if you opened a new dye package to do the new dyeing. Dyes are packaged in batches, and batches have a history of changing slightly over the years. Before panic sets in, ask your rug hooking friends to see if they have a package to spare from the earlier batch.

The next time you buy dye, dye small samples of it to compare to older samples. This will allow you to see if there will be any problems before you start using the dyes for a hooking project (see the section below on dyeing Cushing samples). Or combine several packages of each color in a container. I empty several packages into wide-mouth plastic bottles for future use.

It is also possible that the wool is the cause. The initial material might have been an old white flannel skirt from Aunt Milly, and now all you have is a remnant of white that you found in a barrel at the Dorr Mill Store.

Regardless of the cause, what is the cure? Mix up the formula and dye a small sample of the new wool to make sure you'll be successful. Then mix up the dye you need for the large piece but only put 3/4 of it in the dye pot. Withhold some until you are sure of the color. If the wool needs to be a lot darker, add the rest of the dye mixture. However, if the color needs to be adjusted just a little, you can add small amounts gradually. If you put all the dye in at first and the wool gets as dark as you want but the color isn't right, you won't be able to add anything to it to adjust the color, because no matter what you do, you'll only make the color darker.

Wet a sample of the wool that you are trying to match and compare it with the in-process wool. Squeeze a little corner of each together so that you can see how close you are to matching them. I have a tendency to remove the wool a bit too soon and I end up having to put it back.

Dyeing should be an adventure, not an occasion for alarm and anxiety.

If you get an exact match before the dye bath clears, remove the wool to a resting pot with clear water and 1/4 cup of vinegar in it. Boil that water to set the color. Don't throw away the solution in the original pot until you finish setting the color and can compare it once more to the sample.

As soon as you get a new shipment of dyes, dye small samples for comparison to older samples. This will allow you to see if there will be any problems before you start to use the dyes in formulas.

Dyeing More Than a Yard

When you need to dye more than one yard of the same color and you want consistency of color for the whole lot, take a few minutes to break the dye job down into amounts that you know that you and your pots can handle. For instance, I recently dyed 3 yards of a color. I decided to dye 1 yard at a time because the formula was written for 1 yard, and my pots could easily handle that much material. I measured out all the dye at once in 3 separate beakers. Each beaker held the dye for 1 yard. This meant that I could dye 1 yard right after another without having to stop to measure dye.

I could have easily divided the formula in half and dyed 2, 1 1/2-yard batches. This approach saves time, but you must remember to increase the dye if you use more wool than the original formula is written for. For example, say the formula is written for 1/2 yard of wool and you want to dye 1 yard; you must double the dye that you use. On the other hand, if you only want to dye 1/4 yard and the formula is written for 1/2 yard, then you need only 1/2 of the formula.

Change to liquid measuring if you need to cut formulas and dye spoons won't permit you. For instance, dye spoons don't have a 1/3 teaspoon increment, but you can mix the dye formula in 1 cup of liquid and use 1/3 of that to get the proper amount of dye for your yardage. In metric terms that would be 80 ml from 240 ml (1 cup). See the equivalency chart in the appendix for help with dry and liquid fractions.

Dyeing Cushing Samples

Color consistency, be it for large quantities of material or for matching a previously dyed piece with a new one, is at the forefront of many a rug hooker's mind. To better understand color, and to establish a personal reference guide, I took on a special project early on in my rug hooking career, one I'd advise you to take on, too. I systematically dyed samples of each Cushing dye. Since I didn't have an endless supply of white or natural wool to dye for this project, I had to do a little figuring. I had small children at that time, so there were dozens of empty baby food jars in my house. And, because I bought wool by the pound, I had odds and ends of white wool not big enough for regular swatches. So I dyed my small pieces of wool in my little jars.

The formula I used was the same for all the samples. I derived it by considering the amount of wool dyed by a published formula and then reducing that amount to what I had available. I could fit 18 jars in my roasting pan, which worked out to three different 6-value samples at a time. I made sure that similar colors were carefully labeled during the processing as well as at the end.

First I mixed 1/32 teaspoon of dry dye in 1 cup of boiling water. Into each jar went 1/8 teaspoon of salt and a 1" x 3" piece of white wool. I processed the wool for an hour, halfway into which I added a tablespoon of vinegar to each jar. Once the wool was rinsed and dried, labels were attached to each group of 6 values, and the samples were stapled together and strung on a chain. It took several months to complete this project because I would buy a few dyes each week until I had all the Cushing colors.

This turned out to be a worthwhile project for a couple of reasons. By the time I had measured out each dye, poured it into the jars, added the wool, stirred it, rinsed each sample, hung each to dry, made a tag, and strung the sample on a chain, the color of each package of dye was indelibly impressed in my mind. I still remember them all. That means that when a new package gives a different shade I am alerted to it right away and dye a sample of the new version. It was also worthwhile because it gave me samples to refer to and use to develop new ideas. Furthermore, I could show others what the different dyes looked like. It's been 30 years since I did that chain, and I still refer to it.

It's OK if you vary dye procedures to fit your needs.

Tips

Here are some other tips that I've acquired through the years. You should start your own notebook of such tidbits, and keep it with your dye recipes.

There are times when, no matter what, the dye bath doesn't completely clear. That has happened to me, and I've heard from other rug hookers with the same problem. Well, that's OK. The two most important things about dyeing have nothing to do with a clear dye bath. The first is that the dye that has been taken up by the wool stays in the wool. The second is that you get the full color of the dye in the wool. As long as the wool is the color you want, and that color doesn't rinse out, it is all right that some dye remains in the bath.

It's also OK if you vary dye procedures to fit your needs. My jar dyeing instructions tell you to mix the dye formula in 1 cup of boiling water. You may find that 1/2 cup is better.

You may like to cut wool up in a certain size for swatches that makes sense to you, but is different from what a formula requires. That's fine, provided you compare your wool's size in square inches with the square inches that the formula was written for. I like 3" x 12" strips, which equals 36 square inches, but not everyone does. When I'm using someone else's formula and my swatches are within 10 square inches of the size suggested in the formula, I know my swatches will turn out all right. If my swatches are quite a bit different I either adjust the formula or adjust the amount of wool.

What I'm trying to get across is that the world won't come to an end if you vary things to suit your druthers. If you have only apple cider vinegar on hand instead of white vinegar, go ahead and use it. But make a note of it because it may make a difference in the color, and you would want to remember what you did. The same holds true for salt. It is always recommended that you use plain uniodized salt, but if all you have is iodized and you just can't wait until you get plain salt, pour it in—and make a note of it. If the dye bath comes to a rolling boil when I told you to keep it at a simmer, just turn down the heat until the water quiets down and continue. If there is wool in the pot at the time, stir it continually to keep it submerged until the dye bath calms to a simmer. The worst that happens is that the wool bubbles up while boiling and the parts that are not submerged will not dye like the parts that are. Also, at a rolling boil the vinegar will boil away faster, so you'll have to add a little more.

Dyeing should be an adventure, not an occasion for alarm and anxiety. With every session at the dye pot you'll learn more and enjoy it more. And don't let dyeing be a solitary pursuit. Later on in this book I'll introduce you to some wonderful students and friends I've encountered through dyeing wool for hooked rugs.

PROJECT

I strongly suggest that you dye gradation samples of all the different dyes that you use as I dyed the Cushing samples. (I did the same with PRO Chem dyes.) Do this sampling even though you may not use gradation swatches in your hooking, because these 6-value samples allow you to see the dye in a variety of strengths. Label and string them on a chain or heavy string for future reference.

Chapter Eight

MY FAVORITE RECIPES

***Floral mat*, 12 $^{1}/_{2}$" diameter, #3-cut wool on cotton warp. Designed and hooked by Maryanne Lincoln. This piece was hooked with colors whose recipes appear in this chapter, such as Antique Rose, Corn, and Dusky Lilac.**

During the last 15 years I have worked more and more with just a few colors of dye, especially when I am developing new formulas. With just red, yellow, blue, and black I am able to dye a complete color wheel of hues from very bright to very dull and from very light to very dark. Sometimes as a shortcut, and for good color mixing, I use Cushing's Orange or PRO Chem's #233 orange to make browns. It pays to learn to mix any color that you need from these primary colors; but it doesn't mean that I never use any other dyes—I have a jelly cabinet full of dyes.

Nonetheless, I choose to use dye colors that are most like the printers' ink colors of magenta, cyan, yellow, and black because they give a fuller range of hues. Crayon-red (fire engine red) is

***Floral chair seat*, 17" diameter, #3-cut wool on burlap. Designed by Pearl McGown. Hooked by Maryanne Lincoln. To hook this seat Maryanne used 8-value swatches dyed with Cushing dyes.**

not a primary color like some people think it is. Rather it is a combination of primary red and yellow. Therefore, bright red-purples and other blends can't be made by using that red because of the yellow already built into it. In contrast, a pure, primary red can mix with anything, which is why I choose to stick with the primaries.

The recipes that follow are the result of years of experimentation. Every time I teach my color course it is clear to me that rug hookers love to see new colors develop and to collect samples and formulas. That's why I'm sharing my recipes with you. The dyes used in these formulas are Cushing's Canary, Cherry, Peacock, Orange, and Black or PRO Chem's #119 yellow, #338 red, #490 blue, #233 orange, and #672 black. I mixed these dyes for the following recipes in 1 cup of boiling water, used the jar dyeing method, and placed 1 strip of 3" x 24" white wool in each jar.

When I am dyeing a color for the first time I like to dye it over white wool because it allows me to see the color unaffected by the color of the wool. After I see the color over white, I can confidently dye it over any color I wish and know what the results will be. You can see my results over white wool in the accompanying swatch photos.

CUSHING FORMULAS

Buttercup

- 3/4 tsp Canary
- 1/128 tsp Cherry
- 1/128 tsp Peacock

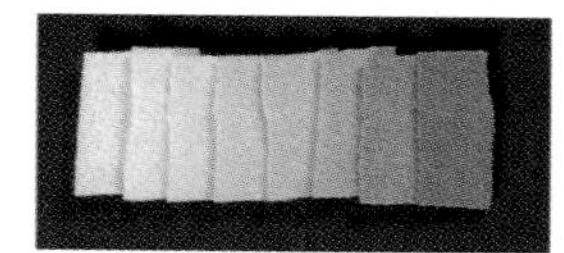

Butterscotch #11a

- 1/2 tsp Canary
- 1/128 tsp Peacock
- 1/64 tsp Cherry

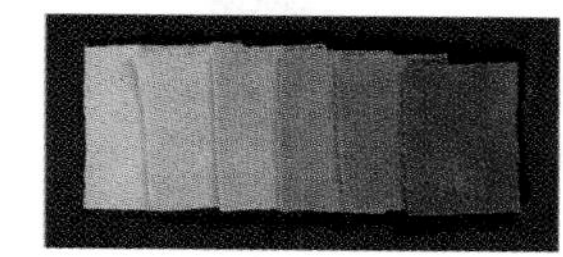

Confederate-Blue

- 1/16 tsp Black in 1 cup of boiling water. Pour this solution into each jar. Next, mix up:
- 3/32 tsp Peacock
- 3/64 tsp Cherry in 1/2 cup of boiling water and add 3 1/2 tsp of this solution to each jar.

Eggplant #9a

- 3/8 tsp Cherry
- 3/8 tsp Peacock
- 1/64 tsp Canary

Foliage

- 1/2 tsp Canary
- 3/16 tsp Peacock
- 1/32 tsp Black
- 1/32 tsp Cherry

Lady Slipper

- 1/8 tsp Canary
- 1/128 tsp Peacock
- 1/128 tsp Black
- 3/8 tsp Cherry

Mahogany

- 1/2 tsp Canary
- 1/32 tsp Peacock
- 1/64 tsp Black
- 3/16 tsp Cherry

Morning Glories #7a

- 1/8 tsp Peacock
- 1/64 tsp Cherry
- 1/128 tsp Canary

Mum Leaf Green #3a

- 3/32 tsp Peacock
- 5/16 tsp Canary
- 1/32 tsp Cherry
- 1/128 tsp Black

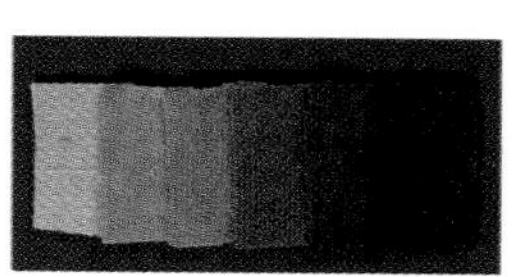

Oak Leaf Gray-Green

- 3/128 tsp Cherry
- 1/4 tsp Canary
- 1/32 tsp Peacock
- 1/128 tsp Black

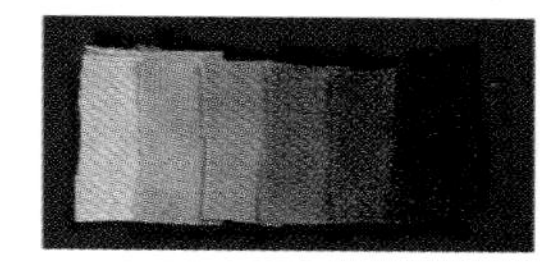

Pink Mahogany

- 1/16 tsp Cherry
- 5/64 tsp Canary
- 1/64 tsp Peacock

Red Grape

- 3/8 tsp Cherry
- 1/8 tsp Peacock
- 1/64 tsp Canary

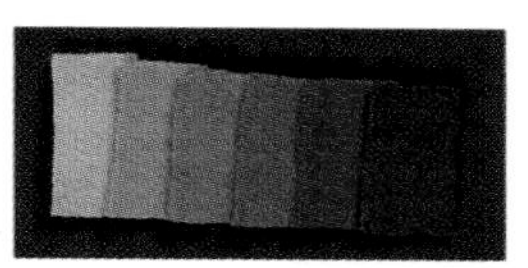

Rich Red #1a

- 5/16 tsp Cherry
- 1/4 tsp Canary
- 1/128 tsp Peacock

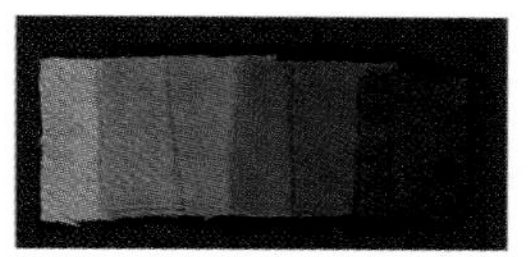

Rusty Orange #2

- 1 tsp Canary
- 1/128 tsp Peacock
- 1/8 tsp Cherry

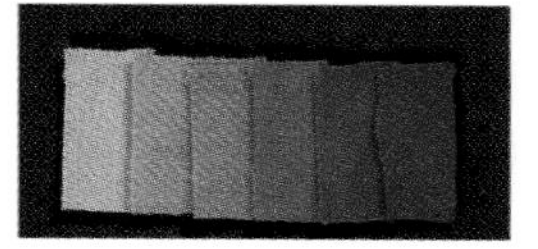

Rusty Tulip #5a

- 3/8 tsp Canary
- 1/16 tsp Cherry
- 1/128 tsp Peacock

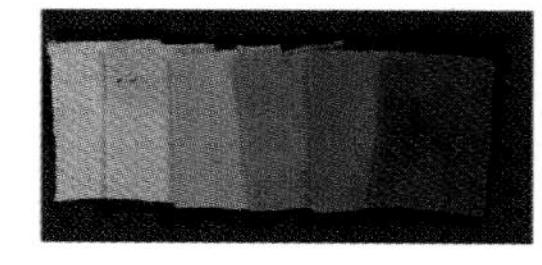

Soft Gray-Green

- 1/4 tsp Canary
- 1/32 tsp Peacock
- 3/128 tsp Cherry
- 1/128 tsp Black

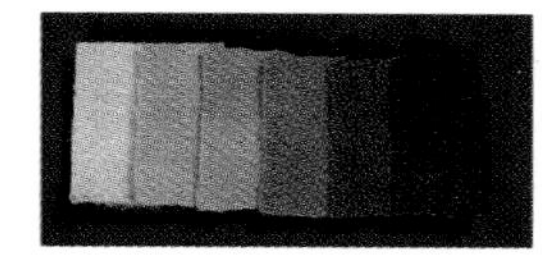

Winter Cedar

- 1/2 tsp Canary
- 1/32 tsp Peacock
- 1/64 tsp Black
- 1/32 tsp Cherry

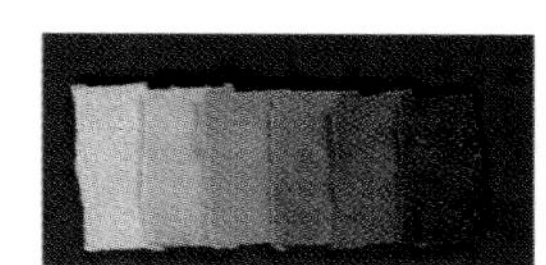

Antique Rose
- 3/32 tsp #672 black
- 3/32 tsp #233 orange
- 3/32 tsp #338 red

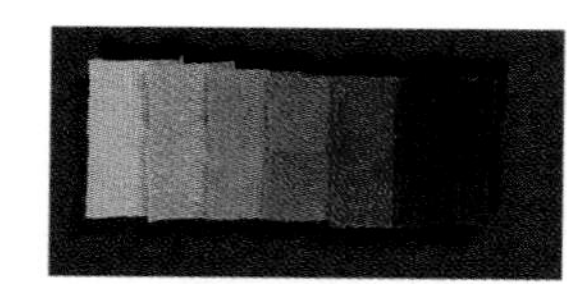

Cardinal
- 1/2 tsp #338 red
- 1/16 tsp #233 orange
- 1/8 tsp #119 yellow
- 1/128 tsp #490 blue
- 1/128 tsp #672 black

Corn
- 3/128 tsp #672 black
- 1/128 tsp #233 orange
- 1/8 tsp #119 yellow
- 3/128 tsp #338 red
- 1/256 tsp #490 blue

Mix 1/128 tsp blue in 1 cup of boiling water and use 1/2 cup to get 1/256 tsp blue.

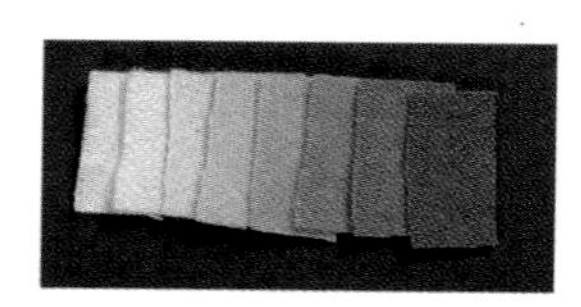

Dusky Lilac
- 3/32 tsp #672 black
- 1/32 tsp #490 blue
- 1/32 tsp #338 red

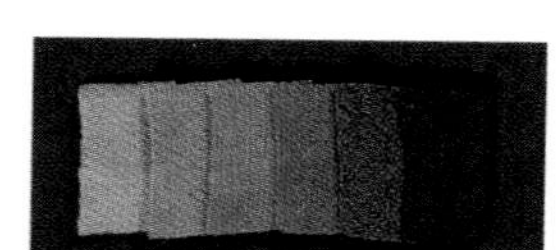

Egyptian Red #2a
- 3/8 tsp #338 red
- 5/32 tsp #119 yellow
- 1/64 tsp #490 blue

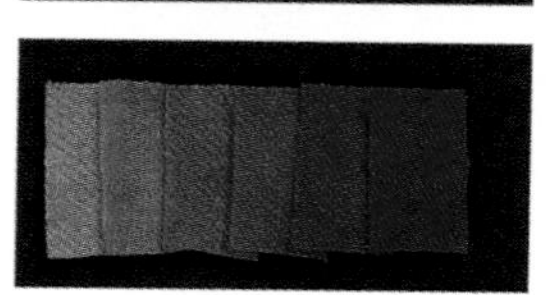

Gray-Blue
- 1/16 tsp #672 black in 1 cup of boiling water. Pour this solution into each jar. Next, mix up:
- 1/16 tsp #490 blue
- 1/64 tsp #338 red in 1/2 cup of boiling water and add 3 tsp of this solution to each jar.

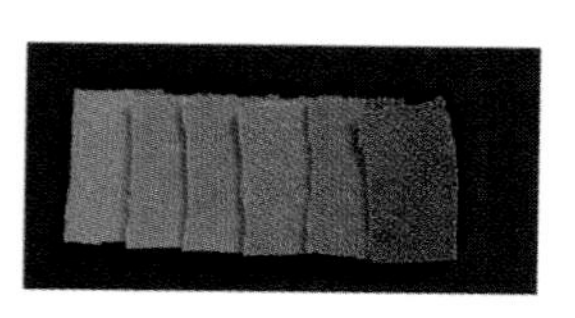

Mahogany
- 1/16 tsp #338 red
- 5/64 tsp #119 yellow
- 1/64 tsp #490 blue

Monarch-Orange #6a
- 3/4 tsp #119 yellow
- 1/8 tsp #338 red
- 1/128 tsp #490 blue

Old Clay Pots
- 1/16 tsp #672 black
- 1/8 tsp #233 orange
- 1/32 tsp #338 red

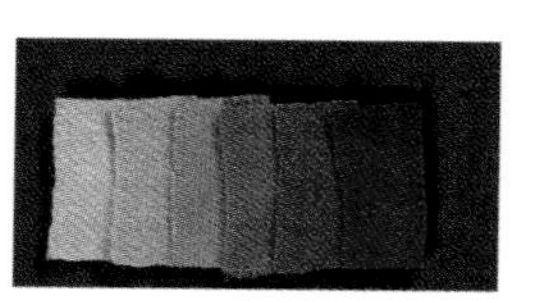

Pansies #10a
- 3/16 tsp #338 red
- 3/16 tsp #490 blue
- 1/64 tsp #119 yellow

Robin
- 1/64 tsp #338 red
- 1/8 tsp #233 orange
- 1/64 tsp #490 blue
- 1/32 tsp #672 black

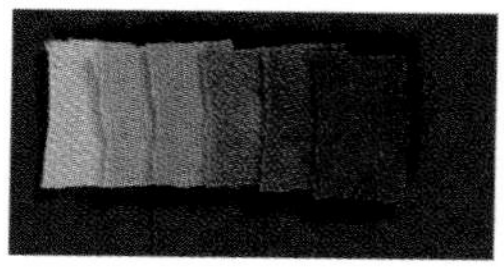

Robin Breast
- 1/32 tsp #338 red
- 1/4 tsp #233 orange
- 3/128 tsp #490 blue
- 1/32 tsp #672 black

Rosewood
- 1/16 tsp #338 red
- 1/32 tsp #119 yellow
- 1/8 tsp #233 orange
- 1/64 tsp #490 blue
- 1/64 tsp #672 black

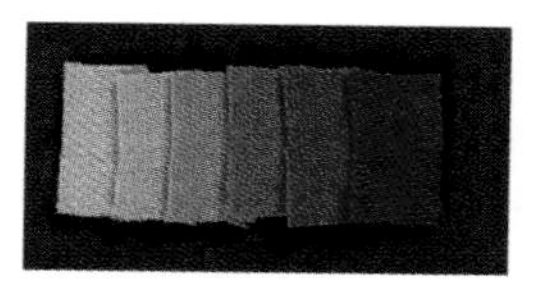

Seafoam
- 3/32 tsp #672 black
- 1/32 tsp #490 blue
- 3/32 tsp #119 yellow

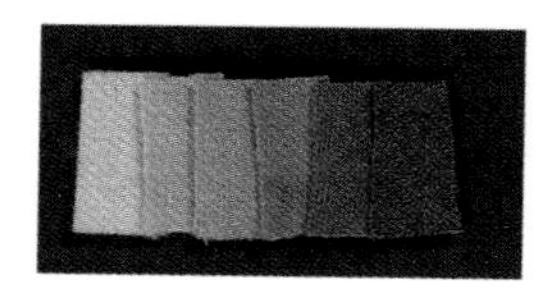

Soldier-Blue #8a

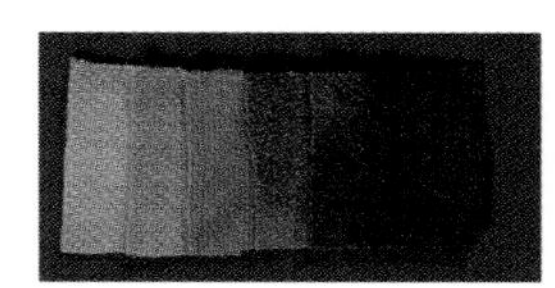

- 1/4 tsp #490 blue
- 1/64 tsp #119 yellow
- 1/64 tsp #338 red
- 1/16 tsp #672 black

Summer-Green #4a

- 3/32 tsp #490 blue
- 3/8 tsp #119 yellow
- 1/32 tsp #338 red
- 1/128 tsp #672 black

Sunflowers #12a

- 1/2 tsp #119 yellow
- 1/128 tsp #490 blue
- 1/64 tsp #338 red

Tropical Foliage

- 1/4 tsp #119 yellow
- 1/32 tsp #490 blue
- 3/128 tsp #338 red
- 1/128 tsp #672 black

Winter Bark

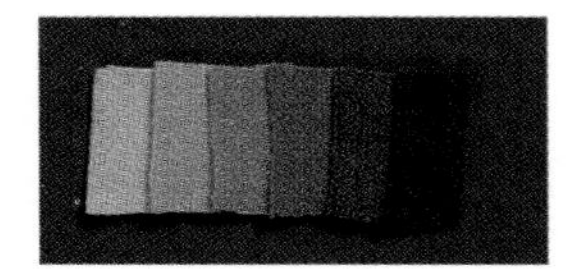

- 3/32 tsp #672 black
- 1/64 tsp #490 blue
- 3/32 tsp #233 orange

Wisteria

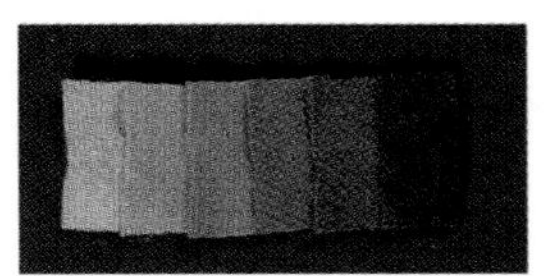

- 3/32 tsp #672 black
- 1/64 tsp #490 blue
- 3/64 tsp #338 red

I hope that, after you've dyed gradations based on a few of these recipes, you'll begin to see other possibilities. For example, if you use my jar method, you'll see that the first value that is poured into a jar is the darkest value, and it takes half of the total amount of dye solution. You could eliminate that value and save that dye by just preparing 1/2 of the formula. On the other hand, if you want a value darker than you see in the recipe's swatch, mix twice as much dye as the formula calls for and then pour it into the jars as usual. The darkest value would now be darker than it is with just the regular formula. Other ways to alter the gradations include adjusting the color and size of the wool that you use. If you put more wool in with the same amount of formula the values will be lighter. If you use less wool the values will be darker. Just remember to put the same amount of wool in each jar if you want an evenly spaced range of values from dark to light.

Rug hookers love to see new colors and collect formulas.

Chapter Nine

DYEING BY EYE

***Pear With Blueberries*, 9 1/4" x 5 3/4", #3-cut wool on burlap. Designed and hooked by Maryanne Lincoln.**

Over the years I have traveled all across the country to teach rug hooking classes and my color course. On many occasions I have been invited to give special dye presentations at different types of rug hooking functions. While jar dyeing is a great way to dye swatches at home, it sometimes takes more time than I have with my students. Hour-long seminars don't give me extra time to wait for results or adjust formulas. Fortunately, necessity, the mother of invention, has found a solution—dyeing not with jars, but dyeing by eye.

I can't remember when I started dyeing by eye. It must have been at one of those short presentations that I do. I mixed up some liquid dyes and put them in plastic squeeze bottles (the kind ketchup comes in at hot dog stands). With a pot of water and vinegar boiling on a hot plate, I started squirting colors into the pot. A little red went in, then yellow, and a drip of blue and black. Within minutes of tossing wet wool into that pot I had a lovely piece of dyed material. It was easy to dye this way, and the results were just what I wanted. After fiddling around for a few minutes, I realized that I could repeat what I had done and adjust the color as need be. I was so excited about this simple process and its rapid results that I immediately started teaching it to others.

Using this dyeing technique not only makes it quick to dye wool but also quick to pack for a class. Now when I travel to teach I need only basic dyes, a wetting agent, vinegar, squeeze bottles, a soaking pot, and one self-contained dye pot.

For years I did this kind of dyeing in a 2-quart saucepan on a convenient, but slow, hot plate. One time I went off on a hooker's holiday with everything to dye with except the hot plate. When I realized what I had done I went charging off to a local department store to get one, but the only thing they had was an electric cooking pot (the brand name for mine is a Rival Chef's Pot). Now I use this self-contained hot pot whenever I travel to teach. It has a temperature control like an electric frying pan but is deep enough to dye 1/2-yard hunks of wool. It gets hot fast and is portable. It makes dyeing more fun not only for the students but for me, too.

The Process

No one told me how strong to make the dye solutions that I started with. So I decided to always make a standard solution of 1 teaspoon of dry dye to 2 cups of boiling water. It has been suggested to me that 1/2 teaspoon in 2 cups of boiling water would be more stable (less apt to separate out because there are fewer dye particles). However, you should do as you wish—just always do it the same way each time you mix up more dye.

I measure the dry dye into a 2-cup glass measuring cup, add a teaspoon or two of tepid water to stir into the dry dye, and then pour in 1 cup of boiling water. I stir the solution briskly to

***Fruit placemat,* 20 1/2" x 14 1/2" #3-cut wool on linen. Designed by Florence Petruchik. Hooked by Maryanne Lincoln. All the wool for this mat was dyed by eye by Maryanne.**

I got excited by this easy process and its rapid results.

thoroughly dissolve the dye and then add hot tap water to the mixture up to the 2-cup line. This means the solution is not boiling hot when I then pour it into the squeeze bottle. (Squeeze bottles that handle boiling water are available from PRO Chem. See the glossary for PRO Chem's address.) I use 5, 16-ounce bottles when I dissolve 1 teaspoon in 2 cups of boiling water, one for each of my favorite dyes—red, yellow, blue, orange, and black. When I'm ready to add the dye to the pot I cover the tip of the bottle and shake the solution a bit.

As always, I put vinegar in the dye bath—1/4 cup. After the bath water clears I leave the wool in the pot with the heat off and the lid on for up to 20 minutes.

There is a time and place for each type of dye procedure. When I want precise swatches with multiple values I plan to repeat, I use the jar dyeing procedure. If I want colors for fruits and vegetables I do scrunch dyeing, sometimes with a formula and sometimes dyeing by eye. If I need to dye backgrounds, I use a form of open pan dyeing, sometimes with a formula and sometimes dyeing by eye. If I just need a quick color match I dye by eye.

Dyeing by eye may sound like a lackadaisical way of doing things but it really isn't. With practice it becomes easy to repeat colors you have dyed with this technique. It is like learning to ride a bike. You could have always kept those training wheels on your bike, but at some point you just had to let them go. Wasn't it exhilarating to ride off that first time, realizing that you no longer needed anything to hold you up? Your first experience might have been a little wobbly, but each ride after that got smoother and smoother until before long you were whizzing off on your bike like a pro.

The one hitch to dyeing by eye is that you have to be willing to let go of all formulas and precise measurements and replace them with a good eye for color. I urge you to do just that and begin training your color eye today.

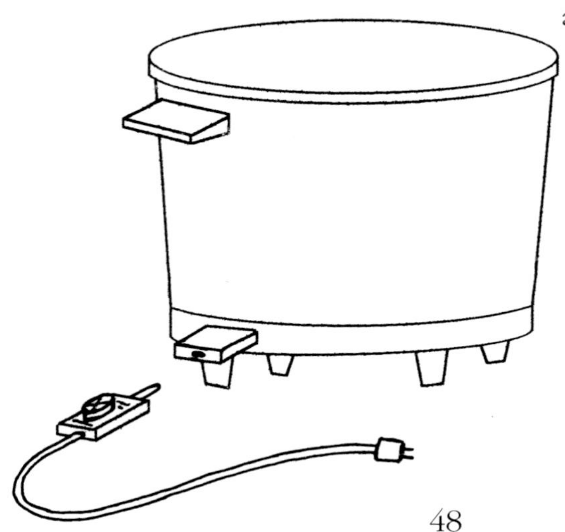

Chapter Ten

STUDENTS, FRIENDS, & RUGS

***Nellie Bird March,* 37" x 27", #6-cut wool on linen. Designed and hooked by Maryanne Lincoln. Each bird represents a teacher present at a rug camp Maryanne attended.**

It was in September 1964 that I attended my first rug hooking class. Earlier, with the help of a magazine article on how to hook, I had tried to make a rug from scratch, but failed. I had no specific skills that would assure me that I would be successful this time except a burning desire to hook a rug, good study skills, a love of needlework and drawing, and a generous portion of patience and persistence. However, my college training was in business economics, not home economics. I was not a trained artist, nor did I know how to dye rug wool.

My teacher for that first course was Mrs. Edna Callis, a woman who became such a fast friend to me that, although I still respectfully call her Mrs. Callis, my children call her Grammie. Mrs. Callis was the perfect teacher for me. She offered the discipline of classroom lectures, blackboard shading lessons, and dye demos that I needed. She guided each of us in the class through our first color planning experiences. Before I took her course I knew nothing about color and less about dyeing. Her instructions were specific when they needed to be, but she expected each of us to also work on our own.

PHOTO COURTESY FLO PETRUCHIK

***Vegetable Rug*, 40" x 28", #6-cut wool on linen. Designed by Florence Petruchik and Maryanne Lincoln. Hooked by Florence Petruchik. Flo and Maryanne's teamwork is evident in both this rug and the vegetable seed packets on page 28.**

Lessons From My Rugs

My first rug, *It's a Cinch* (page 6), was planned in class. Mrs. Callis had us dye white wool in 8 values for all our colors (today I usually dye only 6). The formulas for this rug came from the Lydia Hicks dye booklet *TOD Book I* (self-published, 1957).

Notice that some of the swatches I used in *It's a Cinch* are related to each other—they have the same dyes in them, but in varying strengths. Seeing these relationships was helpful for an inexperienced dyer like me. Mrs. Callis guided each of us through choosing the colors from her sample books.

Ten days after finishing *It's a Cinch* my daughter Kathleen was born. While I was still in the hospital, my husband, Donald, brought a dozen red roses to celebrate Kathleen's safe arrival. The roses were beautiful, my favorite color red, and they inspired me to begin planning to hook the realistic roses on another Pearl McGown design, *Gainsboro*. Mrs. Callis came to visit me in the hospital and I surprised her by asking her to come up with a dye formula to match the color of the roses. She went home with one of the roses, and worked out the formula for use in *Gainsboro*.

Mrs. Callis had taught us to dye an 8-value gradation swatch, which goes from a very dark value to a very light value. However, for *Gainsboro* I needed a swatch that went from very dark blackish red to red, and red is actually a medium value, not a light value. Therefore, I was faced with my first opportunity to be creative with swatch dyeing. Donald and I put our heads together, and between the two of us we came up with a way to do it, which can best be described as double dyeing for in-between values. One day while Kathleen was napping I tried it and it worked.

I mixed up double the amount of formula in 2 cups of boiling water and divided it equally between 2 cups. I used 1 cup to pour off 6 values for a regular swatch in 1 set of jars. I put 1/4 cup of the other cup of formula in a jar with a tight lid and set it aside for future use. After adding water to the remaining 3/4 cup of solution to bring its level back to 1 cup, I poured 6 values into a second set of jars. Now there were two sets of 6 jars with formula. I then proceeded with the jar dyeing method to get 12 values. I labeled the one series of swatches Gainsboro Red Full strength, and the other Gainsboro Red 3/4 Strength. It has been more than 30 years since I dyed that wool, but the rug's roses still look good.

Gainsboro Red swatches, both full strength (top) and 3/4 strength.

Gainsboro was a test of my budding skills as a dyer. *Farmer and Wife* was created just for the fun of it. My husband had just finished remodeling the kitchen and his work inspired me to make a rug to celebrate. I wanted to dye a background using PRO Chem's blue so I could see how it would hold up to fading over time. I also wanted to try dyeing selvages and using them in a background.

I made up a story about the rug as I went along. Donald is standing there admiring his handiwork. I, in the meantime, am upset because the cat has been playing with a mouse. Our dog, Samantha, is staring at the cat, which is what she does best. The goose, chicken and cow are memories from my childhood. When I was small my dad kept cows, and one of them was always reluctant to return to the barn. When we'd guide her home this is the part of her I'd see. That's the tail end of my story. Or is it an udder tale?

***Gainsboro*, 59" diameter, #4-cut wool on burlap. Designed by Pearl K. McGown. Hooked by Maryanne Lincoln. Double dyeing for in-between values was done for the roses in this rug.**

Becoming a Teacher

From the time I finished my first rug with Mrs. Callis, I wanted to become a rug hooking teacher. Since there was so much to learn, I reasoned that it would take years before I would be prepared to teach just the basics. Mrs. Callis advised and supported me along the way.

***Nighttime on Main Street,* 19 1/2" x 11", #5-cut wool on burlap. Designed by Jane McGown Flynn. Hooked by Maryanne Lincoln.**

After five years of being a student, I agreed to take over Mrs. Callis's class. As the years passed I took on more adult-education classes and participated in McGown Teachers Workshops. This led to teaching at McGown Guild rug schools in Maryland, California, and New Hampshire and other rug camps around the country.

When my youngest son was about a year old, in 1970, I accepted a few private students at my home in Norwood, Massachusetts, although I really didn't have the room in my house. A year later we found a home in Wrentham with lots of classroom and dye kitchen space and we moved. Thanks to my husband, who built a dye kitchen for me and added lighting, I eventually was able to teach exclusively in my home and at rug camps.

Teaching at the Texas Rug Camp in 1991 inspired me to hook *Nellie Bird March*. After the first day of teaching, all the teachers relaxed before retiring. Someone suggested, and we all agreed, that we should form a Tired Teachers Association (TTA). Lois Dugal even came up with an idea for our retirement home. She referred to the residents of the proposed home as the Roundhouse Nellies. Each bird on my rug represents one of the original TTA members.

The first bird I hooked represents Jane King. Because she was a part-time resident of New Mexico, I put a cactus and mountain by her. Lois Dugal was my teacher at that camp, and since she is from New Hampshire and likes to write poetry, I put her on skis and gave her a poetry assignment. Betty Laine is from Canada, so I gave her bird a special wing shape, but what's best about this bird is that it is dyeing pantyhose for Grenfell rugs, just like Betty does.

Flo Petruchik loves flags, flags, flags (and tennis). Can you guess which bird is Flo? Pat Chancey was the director of this Texas camp and greeted everyone as they arrived. Her wing is special, too. Last of all these silly birds is mine, all decked out in rainbow colors and offering my primary dyes to everyone.

Many rug camps have come and gone since that TTA gathering at Lazy Hills, but I don't believe there will be any other as memorable. I am happy to have commemorated it in this playful rug.

The hope of finally mastering the ins and outs of color is my incentive to keep moving forward.

Students & Friends

Students inspire and encourage teachers. Some, we hope, go on to do greater things. Several of my pupils stand out in my mind.

In 1972 Anne Palmer became one of my first students, and she is still with me. Anne hooks beautiful rugs with a #3 cut. She is careful and precise, and her rugs show it. Also that year Lorraine Pelletier began lessons with me. She still hooks and has brought her daughter, Diane, into the fold.

A few years after Lorraine started classes with me, Diane Stoffel found her way to my doorstep. She had purchased a Colors by Maryanne swatch and found my phone number on its tag. In 1983 Diane took my three-day color course, after which she went home and dyed the 36-sample color wheel I told the class about. Lib Callaway's *Polly* (page 15) is the result of that course. Diane's technique is flawless, and she has one of the keenest color eyes I know.

My friendship with Pat Chancey started at the McGown Northern Teachers Workshop, and has grown since then. A few years ago she asked me to help her hook a realistic red rose. I charted it out for her, provided the dyed swatches, and watched over her as she hooked that first rose. She fussed and fumed and sputtered all the while, but once she finished that rose she went on to hook a whole rug of roses (*Marie*, page 54) and taught that rose to others.

Ronnie Roisman was in my first class at the Green Mountain Rug School in Vermont. Ronnie had her own ideas about color, so working with her was challenging. She attended more of my classes and our friendship grew. One of her rugs, *Collinot* (page 35), was featured in *A Celebration of Hand-Hood Rugs V* (*Rug Hooking* magazine, 1995). I encouraged her to become a teacher, and when I met some of her students two years ago I was happy to find that they loved her.

I met my student and assistant Flo Petruchik in 1972 when I was dragged, half-dressed, out of a ladies room to meet her. I was dressing for the first McGown Guild rug show when Flo,

From the time I finished my first rug with Mrs. Callis, I wanted to become a rug hooking teacher.

excited at finding out a rug hooking teacher lived near her, insisted on meeting me. She began classes as soon as we both returned home, and by 1983 she had become my right-hand man. Flo has assisted me with swatch dyeing for years and has accompanied me to countless workshops. She was the reason the rug schools that I ran were as well received as they were. The vegetable rug she hooked (on page 51, which I hooked as individual seed packets on page 28) is a design she and I worked on as a project for a class of mine. I would not be who I am today if I hadn't met Flo at that rug show. Thanks, Flo, for all your help.

For another class Flo and I worked on a Jane McGown Flynn design, *Nighttime on Main Street.* I didn't have time to develop a color plan for the entire piece, so I shrank the design and hooked a night scene. That way all the houses could be the same color and I could dye a special sky using 4 parts #672 black and 1 part #490 blue. To keep from getting bored hooking all that black I made up a story about the town. It seems that one of the shopkeepers is appearing in court tomorrow. Both his tailor and his lawyer are burning the midnight oil to prepare. An owl on top of one of the buildings keeps a watchful eye over the proceedings. By the time I finished the story I had finished the mat.

A Final Thought

As you can tell, rug hooking has delighted me for decades, presenting me with stimulating, creative opportunities and inspiring, fantastic friends. I've found that the study of color is perpetually rewarding. The hope of finally mastering the ins and outs of color is my incentive to keep moving forward.

I have given you enough information here to get you moving toward a better understanding of color. Repeat some of what I have done to make sure that you comprehend it. Then use this basic information to work up some ideas of your own. I hope you find as much delight in your dye pot as I have in mine.

***Marie*, 28" x 45", #3-cut wool on burlap. Designed by Jane McGown Flynn. Hooked by Pat Chancey. Mayanne helped Pat dye and hook a rose, which led to the creation of this rug.**